JEWISH HOMETOWN ASSOCIATIONS AND FAMILY CIRCLES IN NEW YORK

The Modern Jewish Experience
Paula Hyman and Deborah Dash Moore, editors

Edited with an Introduction and Afterword by
Hannah Kliger

JEWISH
HOMETOWN
ASSOCIATIONS AND
FAMILY CIRCLES IN NEW YORK

The WPA Yiddish Writers' Group Study

Indiana University Press • *Bloomington and Indianapolis*

"Jewish Landsmanschaften and Family Circles in New York," prepared by the Yiddish Writers' Group of the Federal Writers' Project, Works Progress Administration in the City of New York, is published here by permission of Municipal Archives, Department of Records and Information Services, City of New York.

The paper used in this publication meets the minimum requirements of American National Standard for Information Sciences—Permanence of Paper for Printed Library Materials, ANSI Z39.48-1984.

Manufactured in the United States of America

Library of Congress Cataloging-in-Publication Data

Jewish hometown associations and family circles in New York : the WPA's Yiddish Writers' Group study / edited with an introduction and afterword by Hannah Kliger.
    p.   cm. — (The Modern Jewish experience)
  Includes bibliographical references and index.
  ISBN 0-253-33128-5
  1. Jews, East European—New York (N.Y.)—Societies, etc.—History.
2. Jews—New York (N.Y.)—Families—Societies, etc.—History.
3. Immigrants—New York (N.Y.)—Societies, etc.—History.
4. Yiddish Writers' Group (New York, N.Y.)—History. 5. New York (N.Y.)—Ethnic relations. I. Kliger, Hannah. II. Series: Modern Jewish experience (Bloomington, Ind.)
F128.9.J5J574   1992
974.7'1004924—dc20   91-26514

1 2 3 4 5 96 95 94 93 92

Contents

Illustrations follow p. 15

For my parents,
with gratitude for their love

PREFACE

The rewards of research often come to us in a variety of forms or in unexpected ways, and the dilemmas of the scholarly process are wont to yield our most coveted discoveries. This book is the product of such a search, characterized by unanticipated encounters along diverse and previously uncharted paths for studying the communal responses of East European Jews in their adjustment to American society.

Persons sharing common origins in an East European city or town are referred to in Yiddish as landslayt. This term is also the designation for individuals who join formal organizations of compatriots from the same birthplace. These mutual aid societies or beneficial associations are commonly known by their Yiddish name, landsmanshaftn. Beginning in the 1800s, immigrants created the landsmanshaft to pray together, provide financial assistance and insurance benefits, to offer traditional burial, to send aid to the hometown, and in order to have a social center for meeting fellow townspeople and friends—the landslayt. But landslayt is also a word that encompasses an overarching relationship, a compelling desire to identify and affiliate with other Jews. Whether we are considering the specific appellation for members of immigrant hometown clubs or the more generic usage of landslayt connoting connectedness to a people, the authenticity and persistence of these bonds must be explained.

This book is not only about the enduring, albeit dynamic and ever-changing, nature of Jewish identity. It is also about the durability of texts that document this development. With regard to the landsmanshaft world, which in the early decades of the twentieth century drew one of every four Jews in New York City into its ranks, evidence of the activities of this vast network of voluntary associations is not easily located.[1]

More than half a century ago, the first large-scale effort to uncover and describe the working of the landsmanshaft sector was attempted by a group of Yiddish writers. In 1938, under the auspices of the New York City Unit of the Federal Writers' Project of the Works Progress Administration (in July 1939 the name was changed to the Work Projects Administration), a major study of landsmanshaft life was launched by the Yiddish Writers' Group or Anglo-Jewish Group under the direction of Yiddish writer, journalist, and teacher Isaac E. Rontch. Also in 1938, the group published results of their research in a Yiddish-language volume, *Di yidishe landsmanshaftn fun nyu york* (The Jewish landsmanshaftn of New York). A book describing Jewish family clubs, *Yidishe familyes un familye krayzn fun nyu york* (Jewish families and family circles of New York), followed in 1939. Together, these two works provided a unique portrait of Jewish immigrant life in America during the early years of this century.[2]

Around the same time, in 1938, Maurice Karpf's *Jewish Community Or-*

ganization in the United States was issued. Although Karpf occasionally mentions landsmanshaftn and family circles, the few paragraphs describing their functions leave the reader with the impression that what there is to say about these groups could hardly fill two full pages, let alone two lengthy texts. And the scant information which Karpf includes in his report is rather unspecific. "The number of these societies," he says, "which are found in all cities with a large Jewish population, is not known, although it is estimated that there are several thousand of them."[3] He notes the existence of family societies, but claims there is "no information" on them.[4]

How then, we must ask, did Rontch and his coworkers manage to produce findings on approximately 2000 organizations that participated in the survey conducted by the Yiddish Writers' Group, including 112 family circles and cousins' clubs? In addition to the two printed volumes, a third on the portrayal of America in Yiddish literature was being compiled, and a draft of an English manuscript, *Jewish Landsmanschaften and Family Circles in New York,* drawn from the two Yiddish volumes, was in the process of being edited and readied for publication. This accomplishment is also noteworthy, as Rontch points out in his memoirs of the time, because "the Yiddish group, in spite of so many hardships, had succeeded in completing two books in less than two years. The other groups, with larger staffs, and with all conveniences, were working on their first book for . . . four years."[5]

Fifty years have passed since the publications resulting from the pioneering WPA study were printed. They were exceptional and original contributions in their time, and they remain indispensable sources. Extracts, particularly from the book on landsmanshaftn, are frequently cited and borrowed. In general, however, the two Yiddish sources are inaccessible: first, because few copies of these books remain, and second, with the exception of one short summary which appeared in the *Jewish Social Service Quarterly* in 1939, this work did not apppear in translation.[6] The anticipated English-language rendition, *Jewish Landsmanschaften and Family Circles in New York,* was never published. The purpose of the present book is to make available this long-forgotten document on the history of Jewish hometown associations and family clubs in New York.

In conducting my own study of landsmanshaftn in the 1980s, I was patently indebted to the content and the product of the inquiry which Rontch had formulated and executed. But I was equally drawn to the idea of it all—the collaborative creativity of a team absorbed with the charge of documenting the common folk of this country. Admittedly, a romantic fascination. After all, Ann Banks reminds us in *First-Person America,* her book of life history narratives culled from the Federal Writers' Project collections, that those writers "who collected the stories were themselves victims of the Depression . . . [with] a salary of about $20 a week."[7] Furthermore, they were destined to "become a convenient target for conservative attacks on the New Deal," and the Federal Writers' Project was criticized, cut back, and finally completely discontinued, bringing to an abrupt halt many projected publications.[8]

A summary of the achievements of the Federal Writers' Project by Daniel M. Fox alerts us to approach this productive cultural experiment, never before or since duplicated, realistically. We must remember, he warns, "the relation of the individual writer to the bureaucratic tangle, the political snarl and the ideals of the Project administrators."[9] Still, it was an exciting effort, a chapter of American history in which, as one observer notes, "writers of the Depression years provided their countrymen with a foundation for national confidence," giving a voice to America's minorities, including the Jews.[10]

We will probably never know the full story of the circumstances which led to the rise and fall of the Federal Writers' Project, which had once employed 6500 workers around the country. When it was disbanded, the written materials and the vast amount of paperwork which this government-sponsored work relief program had generated were hastily scattered among numerous repositories. A guide to the Federal Writers' Project records in archives of state governments and in Washington, D.C., published in 1985 by the American Historical Association, attests to the widespread reaches of the project and the far-flung locations of its files. It also makes evident the disparities in the quality of sorting and cataloguing from place to place.[11]

For my purposes, a visit to the National Archives early in my search for original records of the Yiddish Writers' Group, for example, was not especially fruitful. My ensuing correspondence with the offices of the New York State Archives, and later with the Manuscript Division of the Library of Congress, proved less than promising. Eventually, I discovered in the Library of Congress miscellaneous documentation that ultimately filled in some of the missing gaps in the story I had by then been able to piece together. Particularly helpful in this regard were histories of the Federal Writers' Project by Jerre Mangione and Monty Noam Penkower.[12] Although both of these works noted the contribution of the Yiddish group only briefly, a footnote in Penkower's study caught my attention and sent me to the Municipal Archives of the City of New York. There, in dusty cartons, the story of the Yiddish Writers' Group began to unfold. Research notes, index cards, and memoranda spoke for an even more ambitious undertaking by chief editor Rontch and his staff than I had imagined.

I corresponded with Rontch and met with him and his wife in 1984 in their home in Los Angeles. From Rontch I learned that the funding for the English book had been anticipated, but that because of the demise of the Federal Writers' Project, this translation of selected chapters from the two Yiddish books, like many other endeavors of the project, had been stored away unpublished.

Fortunately, the translation and other documents from the Yiddish Writers' Group were conserved and catalogued in the Municipal Archives of the City of New York as part of a collection of the New York City Unit of the Federal Writers' Project, including materials from the Works Progress Administration Historical Records Survey, which assembled files on the Jews of New York.[13] The helpful guidance of the professional staff at the Municipal Archives enabled me to attempt preparation of an abridged and annotated rendering of the long-lost English-language volume on landsmanshaftn and Jewish family circles of New York.

The opportunity to retrieve the reports that had been disseminated earlier by the WPA and to forge in effect a fifty-year retrospective became a very exciting prospect. I believe that had the English manuscript been fully processed, revised, and published in its time, it would have provided generations of scholars with an important resource for the study of Jewish immigration and Jewish culture and society in the early years of the twentieth century. Additionally, as with other Federal Writers' Project publications that survive, we would have learned about the worldview of the authors who in the 1930s and 1940s constructed this saga.

The present volume makes available for the first time this valuable sourcebook on American Jewish life. Part one addresses the circumstances surrounding the operation of the Yiddish Writers' Group, specifically the groundwork that had been laid for the planned publication of their first English-language book, *Jewish Landsmanschaften and Family Circles of New York.* Part two comprises the text of this document, annotated and slightly abridged. Part three summarizes my findings on Jewish immigrant associations in post-World War II America and discusses the evolution of organizational goals since the 1938 survey. A bibliographic guide to resources for the study of landsmanshaftn and the ethnic organizations of other immigrant minorities and an appendix containing materials from the Yiddish Writers' Group project conclude the volume.

I wish first and foremost to thank the many landsmanshaft participants whom I consulted in the preparation of this study. I am especially grateful to Isaac (Yitskhok) Rontch and Elke Rontch, who graciously welcomed me into their home.

Many generous agencies supported the completion of this book. In particular, I am indebted to the Lucius N. Littauer Foundation for funding the work involved in preparing the manuscript for publication. Tsofi Mitnick was a superb typist and more. The staff at the Municipal Archives of the City of New York, the Manuscript Division of the Library of Congress, the Yivo Institute for Jewish Research, and the American Jewish Archives were extremely helpful. The editors of the Modern Jewish Experience Series for Indiana University Press, Paula Hyman and Deborah Dash Moore, expressed their encouragement and enthusiasm for the merits of the book even before it assumed definitive shape. In the final stages, Deborah Dash Moore provided insightful guidance and good counsel.

Finally, I am grateful to my husband, Rakhmiel Peltz, whose gentle wisdom has carried me along this journey. He is a wonderful partner and friend who understands the treasures of the legacy. With our first-born son Eliezer Haim in our midst, we have even more reason to share hopes for the future.

PART ONE

Documenting Jewish Immigration

New York Jewish Writers and the Works Progress Administration

In January 1939, about midway between the appearance in September 1938 of *Di yidishe landsmanshaftn fun nyu york* and of *Yidishe familyes un familye krayzn fun nyu york* in July 1939, the Yiddish daily *Der tog (The Day)* explored the importance of the immigrant association among its readers. The paper's roving reporter probed a group of six commentators randomly chosen from pedestrians passing on the street and asked them to explain their motive for affiliation with landsmanshaft societies, rather than with other organizations. The choice was distinctively posed and delineated in this way. That in itself was a barometer of the salience of landsmanshaft activity for at least the Yiddish-speaking component of the Jewish community then, and the replies also underlined the predilection for landsmanshaft membership.

The majority of those interviewed notably preferred the landsmanshaft. One M. Shumsky claimed: ". . . . Of course, it is better to join the landslayt. It's special with them: we get together, talk of the old home and share memories, and most importantly we can help the poor landslayt of our hometown." A second volunteered: "Only among *eygene,* one's own. . . . Who of us doesn't warm to memories of the old home? But not all of us have the privilege of returning whenever the longing strikes. When the landslayt get together, however, it feels like home again." One oft-repeated inducement among those partial to the hometown-based fraternity was familiarity and the chance to socialize among friends who "know who you are." Not only connections with the old home were shared, but also concerns about the new one. The drawing power of this comaraderie in the face of new confrontations brought to mind the biblical story of Noah for one of the respondents: "When the flood occurred and Noah took pairs of all the species into the ark, had his landslayt been present, he would surely have invited a pair of them along, too."[1]

The attachments fostered by the landsmanshaft helped immigrants weather the storm alongside fellow voyagers who concurred in their affection for the "old home" and in their absorption with the new land. Self-help and self-preservation were uppermost in the minds of landslayt as they worked first to attend to their basic economic and ritual needs. Later, when the immigration of East European Jews to the United States surged, the newcomers generated a diverse web of landsmanshaft organizations to reflect the fresh requirements of new recruits.

Hometown loyalty intersected with political allegiance, economic status, religious devoutness, gender or age, or even residence in Brooklyn rather than in the Bronx. Consequently, the imminent formation of separate and independent landsmanshaftn to represent these special interests was predictable. For example, the city of Bialystok has been represented by over forty separate landsmanshaftn in America from 1868 to the present, including such groups as the Bialystoker Somach Noflim, Bialystoker Bricklayers Benevolent Association, Bialystoker Young Men's Association, Bialystoker Ladies Aid Society of Harlem and the Bronx, and the Bialystoker Center. In addition to New York societies, Bialystok lodges were also active in Detroit, Chicago, Philadelphia, Newark, Milwaukee, and Canada.[2] Both religious and secular associations of immigrants from the same hometown operated concurrently and as autonomous groups. According to community surveys in New York City conducted in the early years of this century, there were synagogue societies, independent men's associations, women's sections, relief organizations, and locality-based branches of national Jewish fraternal orders.[3]

To this very day, there is no one complete index of the multitude of societies generated in the New York Jewish community. Unlike Polish voluntary associations in Toronto, for example, where the author of a study was able to feel reasonably secure in his ability to canvass every relevant group, creating a total sample[4], the landsmanshaftn of New York have somehow always managed to defy attempts to number or arrange them. Yet, long before the advent of computerized information retrieval, data bases, or telephone polling, the Yiddish section of the New York Federal Writers' Project valiantly coordinated a survey to gather statistical and other information to form a composite portrait of the various landsmanshaft societies in the city.

Rontch described the barriers to gaining entry into this disparate network with its myriad groups, beginning with the fact that very little had previously been published, "no data about their number had been assembled and no record of their activities kept."[5] Among other obstructions, he mentions a very significant one: to ensure "that no outsider may gain admittance to their meetings, an inner guard is still maintained at the door."[6] Other hindrances that threatened to frustrate the project included the recalcitrance of leaders of communal agencies opposed to furnishing their address rosters or identifying landsmanshaft officers because of unfounded suspicions that the mission of the Writers' Group would compete for the revenue of the societies. Another problem was that, once access to the organizations was accomplished, the questionnaires which the project workers distributed were invariably neglected or only partially completed.[7]

The research on Jewish family circles that ensued also met impediments, particularly when the focus of the work turned to one large club which incorporated sixty-eight families. The in-depth case study which was proposed could only proceed with the trust and cooperation of the group. "We knew the matter had to be handled very delicately," Rontch recalled:

> First of all we sent a committee of two workers to see the president, vice-president, secretary and treasurer of the circle. Our plans were presented to them, and they agreed to permit our committee to visit the executive. The executive allowed our committee to appear at a general meeting, and the meeting ratified our plan. The secretary then came up to the project with the seal of the circle, and he stamped our credentials.[8]

But the route was not quite effortless after that, it seems, in "winning the circle over to our side," and it took a new member of the group, "a woman who could make a good impression," to succeed. Rontch confirmed that "as it later turned out, the woman fitted her job perfectly." He explained:

> She had a fine appearance, good manners, pleasant voice and dressed tastefully. Her personality was so winning, that the leaders of the circle invited her to their meetings and regarded her with respect and affection.[9]

At the stage of organizing the writing and analysis, too, ingenuity was required to bring the task to completion, as well as to uphold the principles of discerning collaboration advocated on the whole by the directors of the Federal Writers' Project. In their introductory remarks for such project manuals as *American Stuff,* published in 1937 by Viking Press, or Random House's *New York Panorama, New York City Guide,* and *The Italians of New York,* various administrators expounded on their commitment to the ideal of the "cooperative venture."[10] They clarified how the equitable assignment of field workers, research aides, writing specialists, photographers, and editors enriched each multi-tiered enterprise; some also alluded to the difficulties and creative limitations of this mandate.

Had history taken a different turn, perhaps the Yiddish Writers' Group also would have found its monograph circulated under the imprint of a major publisher. Certainly their efforts, like those of the groups that produced the guides mentioned above, upheld the spirit of resourceful and synchronized apportionment of human talent. We can put together pieces of the modus operandi from Rontch's description of the family circle volume:

> In our new book each writer had the opportunity to work independently on larger chapters. We soon saw, however, that a chapter would have to be assigned to two writers—one to prepare the material, the other to do the actual writing.
>
> When some of the chapters were completed, I found that the work was not altogether satisfactory. We had weekly staff meetings where we discussed the progress of the book, so that each member knew exactly how the work was coming along. The principle of democracy was so fully observed in these editorial discussions, that we even voted on whether the names of the writers should appear over each chapter. The decision was against this, since a number of our writers did not write chapters, and this might reflect badly on them in the eyes of the administration.[11]

As a result of this policy, we do not have assertions of specific accountability for different ingredients of the book. It is, however, possible to determine a nucleus of workers employed by the WPA, a core staff whose names appear in Yiddish and English in the inventory of personnel on the title page. These included A. Abramowitz, M. Bassin, M. Birnbaum, Y. Cohen, S. Daixel, G. H. Garvin, S. Gimplin, E. Greenberg, A. Gurio, Rachel Hirshkan, J. L. Kalushiner, D. Kasher, J. Katz, Lamed Shapiro, M. Vaxer, B. A. Weinrebe (B. Rivkin), B. Weinstein, A. Yudin, and Lillian Zahn.

In the landsmanshaftn volume, on the other hand, the authorship for specific chapters was indicated and the book's table of contents registers the bylines of Lamed Shapiro, M. Blechman, E. Verschleiser, Samuel Schwartz, Menashe Vaxer, B. Rivkin (B. A. Weinrebe), M. Bassin, S. Gimplin, David Kasher, G. H. Garvin, David Sohn, B. Weinstein, A. I. Abramowitz, Boruch Glassman, and Al Gurio.

The files amassed for subsequent projects in English that were being planned show that these teams were joined at different junctures by additional associates. Philip Rahv, for example, assisted in translations from Yiddish to English, as did others. An article by Anzia Yezierska on the National Council of Jewish Women crops up, as does the byline of Nathan Ausubel. Various contributions are attributed to an assortment of individuals who in one way or another, and at some point or another, invested their skills as writers, translators, or researchers.[12]

The dynamic force behind the labors of the Jewish division of the New York City Unit of the Federal Writers' Project, certainly during its most productive phase, on which we are mainly concentrated, was Isaac Elchanan Rontch. From the published record, we know he officially served as chief editor of the two Yiddish albums, but the scope of his responsibilities throughout the Project will probably never be fully known. Rontch, who was a prolific writer of poetry and prose in his own right, died in 1985. He was a sharp observer who composed penetrating journalistic essays that appeared in numerous Yiddish periodicals. He was a regular correspondent for the left-wing Yiddish newspaper, *Morning-Freiheit,* and the scrapbooks of his articles, one of which his widow Elke Rontch generously loaned to me, indicate the range of his interests and the intelligence of his commentaries.[13]

With regard to the era in his career dominated by his involvement in the Federal Writers' Project, a letter dispatched by Rontch to Dr. Jacob Marcus of the American Jewish Archives in 1979 implies that he had composed a 172-page typed manuscript entitled *Writers Must Eat.* "There," he wrote, "I tell the story of the Jewish Writers Project. . . . If you are interested, I will be glad to mail it to you."[14] However, only a short segment of ten pages dealing specifically with the family circles book is present in the Rontch collection in Cincinnati, likely the only chapter he had forwarded.

Thanks to even this brief recapitulation of the events surrounding his tenure with the WPA, we are privy to Rontch's energetic diligence and the extent to which he applied himself in many aspects of the work, and it is regrettable that his full treatise on that era is not available. I have come across only one other short autobiographical synopsis published in English in 1975.[15] Nevertheless, from these documents and other persuasive primary evidence, we can surmise that Rontch was a major actor in (a) envisaging key topics and planning the general work prospectus for the unit, (b) commissioning colleagues to gather specialized relevant materials, (c) allotting turns at different tasks among the office force, and (d) reckoning with the regional and national bureaucracies.

As the official spokesman for the Yiddish group, Rontch was responsible for reporting on the progress of his team to the Administration's directors. In

April 1938, a statement concerning the landsmanshaft book was forwarded to Donald Thompson of the New York City office, ostensibly to explain the need for a deadline extension. Rontch began his memo with a concise and unambiguous rationale for the study. Citing the 1917 New York Kehilla survey of mutual aid organizations, he first presented that group's achievements.

> They worked for more than a year, with a staff of about fifty, and located 1016 societies, supplying data only on 632, sixty-three per cent of the total number.

Then Rontch proceeded to juxtapose their working conditions with his own.

> We gathered lists of Landsmanschaften and the addresses where they meet from leading Jewish organizations of New York. We then compiled a general list of meeting halls and sent out our staff members to visit these societies. Since the work was started in October, 1937, we have already covered 134 meeting halls, and now have complete data on 1487 societies.

He went on to document the ambitious research plan, attached an outline of the projected book, and concluded his note with a clever and convincingly composed bid to ease the task of the Yiddish "poets and storytellers," as Rontch himself identified the staff, with this appeal:

> The fact that we receive many telephone calls and letters from leading individuals and organizations, shows how important our work really is, and we could work more efficiently if we had a secretary, a telephone, more desks, more filing cabinets.[16]

Mediating between various administrators and outmaneuvering some of them was apparently no small matter. Rontch also had to contend with the board of the I. L. Peretz Yiddish Writers' Union, which ultimately agreed to be sponsoring publisher of *Di yidishe landsmanshaftn* and *Yidishe familyes un familye krayzn*.[17] They agreed only reluctantly to this, according to Rontch, as they had earlier when Rontch was nominated as principal manager overseeing the Yiddish Writers' Group.

> The administration of the Federal Writers' Project appointed me editor . . . against my wishes and against the wish of the right-wing socialist I. L. Peretz Writers' Union of New York which supervised the Project. But it involved 26 workers, most of whom would have been dismissed if we had not accepted the proposal giving us six weeks in which to set ourselves up.[18]

The opposition and even antagonism on the part of Yiddish authors in the union did not make Rontch's task easier. For example, in a letter written to the Union, members of the Project's Yiddish staff protested criticism which was publicized in the Yiddish journal, *Der Veker,* that accused Rontch and the entire Yiddish Writers' Group of Communist leanings. In their correspondence, the WPA employees denied these charges and requested an impartial hearing to settle the matter and set the record straight.[19] These objections were usually negotiable. On the other hand, it was much more difficult for Rontch to act as arbitrator on behalf of members of his staff who were being attacked or discharged in the face of what Rontch felt were "constant obstructions on the part of the reactionaries in the Congress and Senate."[20] The criticism of the House Committee on Un-American Activities and the accusations of Congressman Martin Dies could not be turned aside. Rontch and the Yiddish Writers' Group did not escape the dismissals that were mandated as a result of these investigations.[21]

In most other cases, however, Rontch was able to summon up his industriousness and wit to struggle against and prevail upon his challengers, occasionally even to subvert their sentiments in his favor. When necessary, for example, he colluded with his inveterate opponents in the Peretz Writers' Union to successfully revoke unanticipated editorial decrees from the New York Writers' Project office, such as the one "not to write in Yiddish anymore."[22] Injunctions regarding questions of artistic judgments, when they came from local offices or from Washington headquarters, were easier to circumvent or renounce.

From his retelling of the events, Rontch was rather proud of his skill in winning out over some of the protests of his superiors. When it came time to finalize an agreement with the Peretz Writers' Union for publication of the family circles book, for example, Rontch went personally to secure the contract. The executive committee refused his request on the grounds that the union had lost money on the first landsmanshaftn book. The committee disregarded Rontch's insistence that the book had been commercially successful and insisted that another financial backer would have to be found.[23] Undeterred, Rontch plotted the following tactics:

> At a meeting of my staff, I had suggested that we ourselves raise a sum of money. If necessary, each one of us will even borrow a part of it. This money we will offer to lend to the club in order that the book might be printed. In return we will not ask for money but for books. Each of us can sell about ten books at a dollar a book to friends. It was not easy for me to sell this idea to the group. Most of them were family men and they could not afford to give the club a loan out of their $21 a week. Besides, most members of the club earned more in one week than our project writers did in a month. Yet we carried the plan through.[24]

Returning to the union with his request, he received the expected negative response. At an opportune moment, Rontch spread out the bills that had been collected by the relief earners. "Instantly the faces around me changed. The president himself praised our action, and I left the club with a contract and a promise for a check."[25]

Similar predicaments recurred throughout the production of the book. Rontch even anticipated "the usual red tape with the Washington office. I was used to it by now, and I knew that if I waited for Washington, the book would never appear. I gave the material to the printer even before Washington sent its O.K."[26]

This daring step was taken on the presupposition, a not unreasonable one, that surely "there is no one in the Washington office who can read Yiddish." However, as copies of the books were being typeset in the printer's shop in New York, the draft that had been sent to Washington so perfunctorily came back with comments and corrections! "Obviously, someone in the Washington office could read Yiddish, and had read and corrected the entire book in the course of the weekend." Shaken but undaunted, Rontch persuaded the local supervisor that "things were not really as bad as they appeared," and the book was disseminated.[27] Later it was widely praised in the Yiddish press. The *New York Times Book Review* of December 3, 1939, called it "an incisive, authoritative survey of American Jewish life in terms of family behavior."[28]

The Washington bureau, even though it had suggested minor changes and improvements, overall responded favorably. A memo from Joseph Gaer, one of the Washington staff's chief field supervisors, addressed to Henry G. Alsberg, national director of the Federal Writers' Project until 1939, endorsed *Jewish Families and Family Circles in New York* as

> undoubtedly one of the best, and certainly one of the most valuable, books that the Federal Writers' Project has done so far . . . a very original contribution not only to the study of Jewish life and the place of the family in Jewish survival, but also as an [sic] social ethnic discussion that ought to be of general interest.

He concluded that "the workers on this book ought to be congratulated for a job extraordinarily well done," and they should be encouraged to translate it for English readers.[29]

For this commendation and for his satisfactory performance, despite or perhaps because of his cunning in sensing the quirks of human nature and the texture of organizational structures, Isaac Rontch, Identification No. 411274, received a rating of excellent on his employee evaluation of December 1, 1939.[30] This report was issued from the administrative office of Brehon Somervell, New York City's chief of WPA operations, a man of not inconsiderable influence.[31] Indeed, according to the *New York Times* reviewer, it would be "with God and Colonel Somervell permitting," that the completion of the Yiddish Unit's third book on the Jews of New York might be expected in due course, "coordinating in English those parts of the [Yiddish] books which seem of greater interest to American readers."[32]

Nonetheless, the English text was destined to remain in the archives. Perhaps Rontch's private records contain more of the details regarding the unlucky fate of this work, as well as other unanswered queries about the WPA years. Rontch spoke frankly about the urgency of sorting his papers in the note to Marcus mentioned earlier, which he concluded in his inimitable style:

> Elke thanks you for remembering her. Two meetings per day is her meat, but I am
> a vegetarian and would like her to stay home and help me with my archive, which
> I am working on. My 80th birthday demands action.[33]

For the occasion of Rontch's eightieth birthday tribute, Morris Schappes, editor of the English-language monthly *Jewish Currents,* one of the many Jewish cultural institutions with which Rontch was associated, sent greetings to be read at the ceremony in his honor. Schappes lauded Rontch's "literary creativity and activism in progressive causes," and celebrated Rontch's eminence "as an outstanding Yiddish Man of Letters."[34]

This man of letters and the other men and women identified with the Yiddish Writers' Group of the New York City Federal Writers' Project were responsible for turning out what in effect were substantial contributions to American social history. These individuals were not historians or sociologists, nor did they purport to be. Some judgments of their work apply inappropriate standards; other objections are simply fallacious, e.g., the claim that the books merely rehashed previously published secondary sources.[35] On the contrary, the work of this group of Yiddish writers is a model of the kind of ambitious community studies that are typically held up as potent exercises in multidisciplinary data collection, description, and analysis, such as Yankee City or the University of Chicago research teams who used the city as an urban laboratory.

Despite their lack of rigorous academic qualifications, the Project's employees carefully situated their studies of immigrant associations and of cousins' clubs in New York City within a broader context and outlined general patterns in Jewish communal life. The Writers' Project office in Washington praised the family circles manuscript, for instance, and compared it favorably to one of the best known WPA life history publications, *These Are Our Lives.* In fact, the federal bureau hinted that the book outranked its predecessor because, unlike *These Are Our Lives,* "the life histories in this book have completeness and are given in a specific culture, so that the character as a whole is realized rather than one peculiar aspect of that character."[36]

Di yidishe landsmanshaftn fun nyu york had spawned the idea of a conclusive follow-up study of family circles. Preparing the book on landsmanshaftn, the researchers unexpectedly discovered the popularity of family and name societies, a form of social organization modeled after the archetypal landsmanshaft but uniquely geared to circumstances in America. This and other conclusions of the data-gathering phase of the landsmanshaftn project were presented by Rontch in the opening chapter of the first Yiddish volume. A translation of this section by Joseph Katz was printed as a journal article, "The Present State of the Landsmanschaften," in a 1939 number of the *Jewish Social Service Quarterly.*[37]

This article provided a preview in English of the wealth of information contained in *Di yidishe landsmanshaftn*. It presented an overview of the status of 2000-odd landsmanshaftn in New York City that emphasized the diverse population these societies served, as well as their reach into many niches of community life. Additionally, the article presented a typology of landsmanshaftn for categorizing the seemingly endless and uncountable proliferation of groups. The classification system that Rontch and his coauthors engineered highlights recurring patterns and pertinent themes and serves as a reference point. The WPA investigation demonstrated that the number and heterogeneity of New York landsmanshaftn could be sorted according to identifiable markers of congruent organizational behavior.

From their outset, the landsmanshaftn understood that their aims were not only to guarantee former neighbors from an East European hometown such basic needs as the right to traditional Jewish burial, financial subventions and medical benefits, or a place to seek refuge from loneliness. The town-specific identification was the salient tie that brought former residents of a particular locale together, but it was soon counterbalanced by significant factors in the new country of settlement. As a result, we find multiple branches of the same town-based community transplanted in the new world.

The ways in which landsmanshaftn functioned as benevolent societies for European Jews newly arrived in the United States mark these groups as heirs to age-old Jewish communal values emphasizing self-help and philanthropic practices. In the past, they actively raised funds for the upkeep of institutions in the hometown. Today, they also contribute generously to projects in Israel.

The obligations and privileges are formally stated in the official membership handbooks, the landsmanshaft constitutions, but trends in the creation and interpretation of the guidelines found in these documents indicate shifting preoccupations for newcomers and their children. I would argue that this development constitutes the natural progression of ethnic group life in general, which necessarily involves a constant and dynamic search for new cultural identities and their expression.

For the immigrant organization, this adjustment occurs in several spheres such as in language change, in the adoption of formalities of American fraternities, and in organizational responses and agendas. The criteria for affiliation are extended beyond like-minded landslayt from a common European locale to include a more far-ranging field of potential members. So, too, are the limits of organizational platforms stretched to accommodate fresh imperatives. The ongoing task of these groups and their leaders in reconciling American and East European Jewish identities was complex and puzzling to the participants themselves: they claimed special attachments to Jewry's East European past, yet saw themselves as members of the American Jewish citizenry.

One major contribution of the 1938 New York WPA study was to point to the level of complexity within the landsmanshaft world and the variety of its activities. A contemporaneous account of Jewish mutual aid societies in

Hartford based on data collected for the Ethnic Survey of Connecticut by the Federal Writers' Project of that state corroborates the role of landsmanshaftn in American Jewish life:

> Paradoxical as it may seem, by affording their members practical training in democratic procedure and leadership, by actively encouraging among them an understanding and appreciation of American institutions which, as we have noted is a cardinal principle with most of them, the societies are also aiding in the process of their Americanization.[38]

The idea of transforming components of the research files compiled by the New York City project into material for an English anthology on Jewish life had surely been considered and debated in various circles before the translation of chapters from the two Yiddish volumes was finally undertaken. Unfortunately, the records that would clarify the decision-making process and bring to life the editorial sessions of the group are very fragmentary. The original interview schedules and the raw data collected by field workers on landsmanshaftn and family circles are similarly unavailable for our inspection. There is little elucidation of the functioning of the Jewish unit in the general histories of the Federal Writers' Project. Some instructive fragments remain, however, through which we can partially reconstruct, or at least catch a glimpse of, the making of the Anglo-Jewish book, as it was called.[39]

For eventual publication in the new condensed translation, "the first book of its kind in English," Rontch circulated a letter requesting proprietors of meeting halls in New York to supply him with a detailed listing of organizations convening in their buildings.[40] This official memo, signed by Rontch as editor of the Anglo-Jewish Group, as the team was also called, and by the then director of the New York City WPA Writers' Project, Frederick Clayton, establishes the new program that would now occupy the unit.

It is not clear which of the writers were engaged with the tasks involved, but an initial sketch enumerates two unspecified members of the group as translators for the proposed book, which was to be evenly divided into three essays taken from the landsmanshaft book and three picked from the one on family circles. A directory of organizations, presumably the result of Rontch's canvassing, and selections from literature produced by and about landsmanshaftn and family circles were intended for the appendix.

That the bulk of the work was finished is confirmed by the presence of several fragile copies of typed manuscripts in New York City's Municipal Archives. They were stored in black notebooks, all virtually identical with the exception of insubstantial revisions pencilled in on some, mainly improvements in spelling and grammatical style. By the time these drafts were submitted, the structure of the text had been expanded from the original outline to two clearly separate sections, one on landsmanshaftn and another on family circles.

The first half of the book was to portray (1) "the present state of the landsmanschaften," (2) "the social role of the landsmanschaften," (3) "non-Jewish landsmanschaften," (4) "the constitutions of the landsmanschaften" and "the souvenir journals of the New York landsmanschaften," and (5) "landsmanschaften and the Jewish Conciliation Court of America." Part two of the book was to present (1) "East-European background of the Jewish family," (2) "Jewish family circles," (3) "Jewish family life in New York City" (economic and cultural aspects), and (4) "three generations," an in-depth look at the growth of one clan and the issues affecting its members. A glossary of terms, a directory of Jewish organizations in New York, and an index were to complete the projected 300-page *Jewish Landsmanschaften and Family Circles in New York.*

It would be interesting to know how the content of the new book was finalized, and why certain chapters were chosen over others. The section on family circles was basically an abridged version of the Yiddish original, pared down further by excluding a long chapter on the representation of Jewish family life in Yiddish belle lettres. Some of the more flavorful sections of *Di yidishe landsmanshaftn* were bypassed, namely chapters on the folklore and food traditions indigenous to East European Jewish communities, piquant reports on the activities and meetings of specific societies in New York City, and thoughtful analyses of the function of the landsmanshaftn in facilitating immigration and relief aid. Also omitted were the approximately one hundred pages in the book devoted to literary thematics, easily about half of the entire Yiddish narrative. Interestingly, the chapter which described the lodges of other minority groups (referred to as non-Jewish landsmanshaftn, and listed as Ukrainians, Greeks, Negroes, Irish, Germans, Armenians, Bulgarians, Norwegians, Syrians, Italians, Yugoslavs, Czechoslovakians, Roumanians, Poles, Hungarians, Spanish, Lithuanians, and Chinese) was preserved in the English translation draft. The quality of the data on these different groups is uneven, and although there is no way to ascertain this, it appears the information was based largely on secondary sources.

In the 1938 original, selections had been sifted out from the vast literature produced by landsmanshaftn, such as their souvenir journals, almanacs, memorial books, and periodic newsletters. In addition, extrapolations from the body of classic Yiddish poetry and prose about how immigrant Jews recalled the old home and related to the new one were included. Different aspects of "landsmanness," a term I use to betoken all the different manifestations of the quest for community which participation in landsmanshaftn signifies, were also represented in homegrown examples composed by landsmanshaft members for their own consumption—memoirs, speeches, humorous spoofs and sonnets, and even songs. One chapter of this potpourri, I suspect, was at one point considered for inclusion in the English volume. Boris Glassman's article had been translated from Yiddish by Philip Rahv, but his chapter, entitled "The Landsmann Theme in Yiddish-American Literature," was not ultimately incorporated into *Jewish Landsmanschaften and Family Circles.*

Recommendations about the final form the book should take were forthcoming from various corners; numerous comments that were submitted on the suitability of some of the sections, it seems, were eventually overturned. For example, most of the translations rejected by one reviewer for inclusion in the projected English volume, i.e., on the souvenir journals of the landsmanshaftn, about constitutional documents, and regarding the social role of the landsmanshaftn, did ultimately make their way into drafts of *Jewish Landsmanschaften and Family Circles in New York*, and were intended for eventual publication.[41]

Joseph Katz, the translator of Rontch's summary chapter on the landsmanshaftn, submitted his plan for revising the Anglo-Jewish book at the end of November 1940. "The material has great possibilities," he declared, "if carefully edited and checked." His suggestions were of a sweeping nature, with emphasis on ways of organizing and integrating the materials. His guidelines also urged trimming the three-generational case study of Jewish family life and compressing more of the prose "for an adequately-readable English."[42]

This exhortation was rather mild in comparison with the editorial report issued on 19 December 1940 by W.K.V., or W. K. Van Olinda, who had been reappointed to the New York City project after serving in the central office in Washington. He plainly pronounced, "this is not a commendable piece of English writing."[43] The remarks that followed substantiate the reputation that he had acquired as "a man whose chief forte was punctuation."[44] He wrote at the time: "Grammar is faulty and construction is inept. . . . Too many colons." Continuing, he said that "no attempt has been made to follow our established standards of style, especially in compounding." With dictionary in hand, he reproached the writers and page by page was determined methodically to set them straight. " 'Bar-mitzvah' here and elsewhere. Webster does not hyphenate the two words," he quipped, or he detected that "Webster says 'matzo' is erroneous. Should be 'matzoth'."[45] Could criticisms of this caliber have been influential for the group, or even fateful? The answer, we can hypothesize, is yes, if only because this memo portended the extent to which the projects of the Jewish group would be unceasingly and mercilessly subjected to bureaucratic vicissitudes.

Close to the time when W. K. Van Olinda posted his critique, a staff member of the project, S. H. Steinhardt, supplied Clayton, the New York City administrator, with a list of outside experts from whom comments were being solicited on both *Jewish Landsmanschaften and Family Circles* and another projected book tentatively called *Jews of New York*. Among others, the individuals nominated for this task included Professors Salo Baron and Morris R. Cohen, the research directors at the American Jewish Historical Society and the Jewish Welfare Board, and executives of various national Jewish federations. Principally, the purpose of sending off materials for review was "to convince the would-be sponsor of the importance of putting our books over," so that these individuals would then enlist their respective organizations in the same cause.[46]

One of the reviewers was Harry Schneiderman of the American Jewish Committee. He submitted his commentary, which was by no means pat approval, to Charles Baldwin of the district office that summer, then contacted director Clayton in September to say he was pleased "to see that the project had not been abandoned but that, on the contrary, every effort is being made to bring it to conclusion at the end of the year."[47] This show of support was no doubt appreciated by the Jewish staff, who by this time were unsure if and in what form their book would indeed be issued. Clayton, in his reply to Schneiderman, hinted that the path ahead was not all that clear:

> It is true that we are struggling along as best we can (as you doubtless know, recent cuts in personnel have severely handicapped the project) hoping that the book we are doing will be a creditable performance . . ."[48]

To requests from the staff, by now a different mix of veterans and novices, to clarify his notions about publication plans, Baldwin responded with a series of memoranda. By now efforts were centered on one book, *Jews of New York,* which had become remolded into an epic of over twenty-one chapters. Guidelines were furnished for completion of a full draft, and Baldwin urged his writers "to go out and bring me back a bang-up chapter . . . on the New York of the Jews. . . . This chapter can make or break the book."[49]

He stated his intention to complete the writing around 1 February 1942, "so that we can say we have a manuscript of which we all more or less approve . . . or at any rate, on which we do not gag."[50] In this and in other more direct ways, he expressed his disapproval of the tone of previous editions, presumably counting *Jewish Landsmanschaften and Family Circles in New York* among them.[51] New provisional chapters for *Jews of New York* demonstrated a range from colonial history to crime, Jews in the arts and in sports, education, and the press. The work on landsmanshaftn and family circles which had, in a sense, preceded and perhaps even propelled this bustle of eager writing activity was here relegated to a very small part of a very different kind of story.

Considering the crises that interfered with the operation of the Federal Writers' Project, it is surprising that the New York Unit's Jewish Group survived as long as it did, even in all of its different phases. Its English books were never published, but the source material and manuscripts are part of the legacy that remains. The heart of the enterprise was the unprecedented study by a team of Yiddish writers about New York landsmanshaftn and family clubs. It serves well as a testament to an effort, as the prominent Yiddish journalist B. Z. Goldberg expressed, *"tsu bakenen amerike-bikhlal mit amerike-bifrat,"* when the whole of America was introduced to its component parts, to its very essence.[52]

Offices of the Federal Writers' Project. Unless otherwise indicated, the photographs are from the WPA Federal Writers' Project collection of the Municipal Archives, Department of Records and Information Services, City of New York.

Members of the Federal Writers' Project prepare materials for publication.

Congregation Rodef Scholem on the Lower East Side was the meeting place for a landsmanshaft from Podhajce in the Ukraine.

Synagogue for Jews from the town of Lowicz in the Ukraine.

This building on the Lower East Side provided meeting places for several lands-manshaftn.

Mt. Neboh Baptist church on 114th Street in Harlem was formerly a synagogue for Polish Jews.

Congregation Adas Jacob in Harlem was a synagogue for Jews from Slobodka.

This book stall in the Pennsylvania Hotel in New York City displays posters and books of the Federal Writers' Project. A poster at lower right advertises the Yiddish landsmanshaft book.

Federal Writers' Project books are displayed at the Hudson Library Branch in New York City.

A copy of *Di yidishe landsmanshaftn fun nyu york* [The Jewish Landsmanshaftn of New York], one of two volumes published by the Yiddish Writers' Group.

Members of the Yiddish Writers' Group discuss plans for their study of Jewish family life in New York. I. E. Rontch, director of the group, is seated at center.

I. E. Rontch with I. Fefer, a visiting Soviet Yiddish poet, in front of a Jewish bookstore on the Lower East Side, 1944. Courtesy of the Yivo Institute for Jewish Research.

PART TWO

The WPA's *"Jewish Landsmanshaftn and Family Circles in New York"*

An Annotated Edition Prepared by Hannah Kliger

INTRODUCTORY NOTE

This section reproduces, with the amendments described below, the typescript *Jewish Landsmanschaften and Family Circles in New York,* on deposit in the Municipal Archives of the City of New York and published here with the archives' permission.

The table of contents of the typescript on deposit in the Municipal Archives is reprinted in the Appendix at the end of this book. Readers will note that the numbering of the chapters has been consolidated and that two chapters have been omitted. The original designers of the book divided the text into two parts, one on the immigrant associations and one on the family clubs, with appendices on related themes. The narrative presented here comprises eight chapters numbered consecutively.

A chapter on non-Jewish landsmanshaftn was excluded inasmuch as the topic is not directly germane to the theme of this book. Also, information on non-Jewish hometown associations is available elsewhere, as indicated in the Bibliographic Guide. Nonetheless, the attention paid by the Yiddish Writers' Group to the ethnic voluntary associations of other cultural minorities is noteworthy; it demonstrates the global importance they ascribed to these organizations, beyond the Jewish community.

Also omitted is a brief chapter about disputes that landsmanshaftn members brought before the Jewish Conciliation Court of America, a nonrabbinical court of arbitration founded in New York in the 1920s. The material on the Jewish Conciliation Court has been published separately, within the context of an analysis of the constitutional documents of American landsmanshaftn.[1] A lengthy glossary has also been excluded; many of the terms it contained are defined in the Oxford International Dictionary, Third Edition.

The typescript's transcription of Yiddish names and expressions has been retained in direct quotations. Otherwise, the standard orthographic recommendations of the Yivo Institute for Jewish Research have generally been followed. For the sake of clarity and consistency, *landsman, landslayt,* and *landsmanshaft(n)* are always spelled according to these conventions, except in citing direct quotations that employed alternative forms.

The text given here does not include any of the sections of *Di yidishe landsmanshaftn fun nyu york* and *Yidishe familyes un familye krazyn fun nyu york* that were not in the manuscript *Jewish Landsmanschaften and Family Circles in New York.* However, readers interested in the relationship of the

Yiddish Writers' Group's English version to the two Yiddish volumes can consult the tables of contents of these works, reprinted in the Appendix. My annotations, gathered at the back of this book, compare passages in the English version to corresponding material in the Yiddish volumes, frequently providing additional information from the fuller Yiddish text and from other documents in the Writers' Group archive. All note numbers in the text refer to my annotations.

As for the mode of presentation, in the original Yiddish texts we find summary reports on survey questionnaires and in-depth interviews blended with interpretative essays grounded in archival and secondary sources. These books were based on fieldwork and research data, yet they were targeted to the general Yiddish-speaking public and written in an accessible and readable language. The English manuscript in the WPA files reflects this style, which was both the choice and the challenge of Rontch's group.

The Federal Writers, not only the Yiddish unit, were reproached and reprimanded for their subjectivity and for the frank inclusion of their escapades and their sentiments as integral parts of the investigatory and writing tasks.[2] Today our awareness of the relation of researcher to research topic and researcher to research process is more acute, at least in certain disciplines.

Greater sensitivity to the importance of bringing female experiences into portraits of American social life is another marker of change over the years. To their credit, the Yiddish Writers' Group paid attention to the role of Jewish women in the organizational dynamics of the world they were describing and at one point even considered devoting a special section to the ladies' societies.[3] However, the language in which they wrote retained the bias of the male third-person pronoun, referring to all immigrants, newcomers, or landslayt as *he*.

In the half century since *Jewish Landsmanschaften and Family Circles* was conceived, there has occurred a shift toward a vision of immigrants and minorities as true participants, not merely passive onlookers, in the American dream, who can and must be entrusted as interpreters of their own history. An appreciation for these points of view has grown since, and perhaps in part as a result of, the era of the WPA experiment.

1.

The Present State of the Landsmanshaftn

A Study of the Landsmanshaftn of New York

It is significant that when two Jews who are total strangers meet, the first words they utter in greeting are, "Where do you come from?"[1]

Perhaps they have lived in this country the greater part of their lives. They may have carried away with them bitter memories of their birthplace. Yet, without their being conscious of it, a spark of longing for the old home had been glowing in their hearts throughout the years and the chance meeting is enough to kindle it into flame.

A study of the landsmanshaft societies furnishes a key to this unacknowledged nostalgia, and gives one an insight into the life of Jewish immigrants in America.

Our study differentiates between the landsmanshaft benevolent society and the more common kind of benevolent society. In the former, members usually come from the same home town; their families have known each other for generations; they are tied to each other by mutual memories and sentiments. In the latter, members hail from all parts of the world, and sentiments associated with their past are lacking.

When the landsmanshaft societies in New York were first approached on the subject of this volume, some of their officers asserted that inasmuch as their organizations resembled each other like so many peas in a pod there was nothing about them that warranted detailed attention. Among others who questioned the plan were persons prominent in Jewish communal life. They overlooked the fact that the landsmanshaftn are an integral part of the Jewish community, probably the most prominent quantitative Jewish group in New York.

There is no denying the fact that most of the societies seem rather old-fashioned in their ideas, limiting their activities entirely to the dispensation of sick and death benefits. Meetings are conducted in strictest privacy, their portals being closely guarded against outsiders. Thus, instead of becoming the power that they easily might be in Jewish communal life, both here and abroad, these societies cling to a needless isolation.

From the numerous reports on activities of the landsmanshaftn in the Yiddish press it is apparent that a great deal is going on within these organizations. In recent years the desperate plight of Jews in central and eastern Europe has stirred these societies to organize relief committees in behalf of their victimized brethren in their native towns. Such committees are a good indication of what might be done if the landsmanshaftn recognized their common social interests and utilized their joint power in behalf of the Jewish community, but they are only a beginning.[2]

Number of Landsmanshaftn in New York

Any study of the individual landsmanshaftn is hampered by numerous obstacles. Though landsmanshaftn had existed for more than fifty years, no accurate data about their number had ever been assembled and no record of their activities kept. A number of societies declined to help us in this work, and refused to furnish us with lists of secretaries or addresses of their meeting halls. It proved useless to tell them that in this instance the information was needed for a study and not in order to raise money, that the work had the backing of the United States Government and was sponsored by the Yiddish Writers' Union.

Fortunately, there were a number of exceptions which made it possible to proceed with the work. The HIAS [Hebrew Immigrant Aid Society] was the first organization to furnish a list of landsmanshaftn and their addresses. Others who cooperated were the landsmanshaft federations: the Polish Federation, the Galician Federation, the Rumanian Federation, and the various workers' orders.[3] Valuable assistance was also rendered by the Yivo (Jewish Scientific Institute), the Bialystoker Center and a number of individuals.

Estimates of the number of landsmanshaftn in New York City range anywhere from 1,000 to 10,000. According to Judah Pilch, in a paper on the landsmanshaftn published in Hebrew in the *Yearbook of American Jewry,* New York, 1938, there are approximately 3,000 landsmanshaftn in the United States, with a combined membership of about 200,000, and 950 landsmanshaftn in Greater New York. A recent and comparative study of Jewish communal life in the United States made by Dr. M. J. Karpf (*Jewish Community Organizations in the United States,* Bloch Publishing Company, New York, 1938) shows that the exact number of landsmanshaftn in the larger American cities is not known, and definite information concerning their activities and financial state is lacking.[4]

It was therefore necessary to do some pioneer work. The following types were investigated:

1. Ansheys (landsmanshaft congregations)
2. Independent societies
3. Ladies' aid auxiliaries
4. Landsmanshaft branches of the various fraternal orders

5. Family circles and namesake societies
6. United relief committees

Later on we will discuss each variety.

This questionnaire was submitted to each society by the Anglo-Yiddish subproject of the WPA Writers' project in New York City.

1. Name of organization_____District_____
2. When founded_____Purpose_____
3. How founded_____
4. No. of members at time of founding_____Average age_____
5. Have you helped found other organizations_____
6. Are you a member of a federation_____Which one_____
7. Present membership of your organization_____
8. Membership classification: workers_____
   businessmen_____others_____
9. Present average age_____Per cent of non-landslayt_____
10. No. of American-born members_____Proportion of youth members_____
11. Time of meeting_____Place of meeting_____
12. Do you engage in cultural activities_____
13. Lectures_____What kind_____Theatre benefits_____Where_____
14. Language used at meetings_____Correspondence_____
    Minutes_____
15. Do you pay benefits_____Amt. death benefit_____Sick benefit_____Others_____
16. Amt. of dues in your organization_____
17. Have you your own burial plot_____Amt. paid in_____
18. Have you a printed or written constitution_____
19. Have you published any material_____
20. Have you participated in the raising of funds for the benefit of your native town_____
21. Through what agency: Joint_____Indep_____Others_____
22. Amt. raised until now_____Have you sent a representative to Europe_____
23. What ties do you maintain with the old home_____
24. How much aid have you given the various institutions_____
25. Do you help support any American Jewish institutions_____
26. Which ones_____Amt. contributed annually_____
27. What are your assets_____
28. Is your society: Zionist_____Orthodox_____
29. Are you losing members_____Gaining_____
30. Name of your society_____Address_____
31. Name of interviewer_____Date_____

Three hundred out of 1,000 independent societies declined to divulge the state of their financial assets. Sixty-three out of 257 congregations were equally shy of the question. Often secretaries accepted the questionnaires with the promise to take the matter up at their respective society's meeting, but only 68 out of 621 subsequently replied. After several repeated visits, 224 more responded. The following is a typical reply:

> Gentlemen:
> One of your writers left a questionnaire with me which I promised to fill out, but, as you no doubt understand, a paid official of a society cannot take upon himself alone the responsibility of giving out any information concerning his organization without first consulting his superiors. Accordingly, I brought the matter up on the floor of the meeting and a resolution was passed that no information be given out to anyone. I am therefore obliged to deny your request.
> (Signed)

In a number of cases visiting writers were invited to explain to the assembled members the nature and purpose of their mission. The Galician Federation was kind enough to allot speaking time over its radio program to acquaint the general public with the work being undertaken.

Altogether, 154 meeting places in Manhattan, Brooklyn, and the Bronx were covered. The favored locale of the landsmanshaftn societies still seems to be the East Side. There the Central Plaza Annex rents space to 250 organizations, and the National Theatre building to 175 societies. More Americanized landsmanshaftn appear to favor midtown hotels for their meetings and socials. The family circles usually meet in the privacy of members' homes, as well as in hotels and neighborhood centers.

The first filled-in blank was received in October, 1937; the last in July, 1938.

Two thousand and forty-five landsmanshaftn responded to the questionnaire, and 423 declined to reply, or gave incomplete data. All told, 2,468 landsmanshaftn were canvassed, detailed information being secured on 1,942 societies in the following classifications:

1. Ansheys—290
2. Independent societies—715
3. Ladies' aids—71, and ladies' auxiliaries—287
4. Workers' fraternal orders:
   Workmen's Circle branches—164, women's clubs—63, youth clubs—6
   National Workers' Alliance branches—14, and women's clubs—2
   International Workers' Order (Jewish Section) branches—53, women's clubs—11, and youth clubs—2;
5. Other fraternal orders—23; Ladies' auxiliaries—2;
6. Family circles—112; Namesake societies—45;
7. United relief committees—39; patronati—25;
8. Miscellaneous centers and clubs—18.[5]

Different Types of Landsmanshaft Bodies

The Anshey

The anshey is a religious congregation and the oldest form of Jewish landsmanshaft in New York.[6] Two ansheys were founded between 1862–64, five between 1868–77, twenty-five between 1877–87, and sixty-six between 1888–97. Their locale is on Henry Street on the lower East Side, where more than 100 ansheys may be found within the space of a few blocks. Some ansheys rent space from others. In one two-story building four to five ansheys were found occupying the same quarters. Most of the ansheys had heavy locks on their doors and the investigating writers were obliged to make several trips before they found the sexton or anyone connected with the congregation. Many sextons were reticent about their respective congregations and even declined to furnish the addresses of their incumbent officers.

With regard to the item on "assets," a number of anshey secretaries spoke symbolically of the "dead" or "study of the Torah." The majority, however, were more cooperative. During the religious services the writers were not permitted to make notes. Those without hats were barred. On several occasions the timely arrival of one of the writers helped to make up the needed minyen (religious quorum). On one occasion a writer recognized the sexton as his former melamed (Hebrew teacher) in his native town.[7]

A number of ansheys are primarily concerned with relief work, synagogal activities being secondary. With others, the khevre kedishe (committee assigned to look after the burial rites of members) and the misaskim (their assistants), play a leading role.

The Kletsker Society, for instance, has its own synagogue building. Some clauses in its constitution state:

> Each member is in duty bound to conduct himself quietly and with decency and not wander about the synagogue during the services.

> At the time of special prayers he must refrain from carrying on conversations with others. It is up to the trustees to see that this rule is enforced to the letter.

> No one except the designated cantor may go to the altar without first securing permission from the trustees.

> When two bar-mitzvahs or two weddings occur on the same Sabbath lots must be drawn to determine who shall be the first to read the section of the Torah relating to the occasion. If the choice is between a bar-mitzvah boy and a bridegroom the former gets the preference.[8]

In reference to the aforementioned khevre kedishe, the constitution of that society further stipulates that:

Every 15th day of the month of Kislev the chevrah kadishah is to call a meeting and elect a first and second vice president by means of the ballot. The elected officials must know how to read and write Yiddish.

Every 8th day of Succoth, the last day of Passover, and the second day of Shevuoth the special honor of being called upon to read the Torah before the congregation devolves on the members of the chevrah kadishah. Otherwise the president of the congregation confers the honor upon the highest bidders. In the absence of bidders the president reserves the right to distribute the honors among those of his own choosing.

The head of the chevrah kadishah is held responsible for the rules governing the maintenance of the congregation's cemetery.

Every 15th day of the month of Kislev the chevrah kadishah is to tender a dinner to its members. . . .[9]

Societies

The sick-benefit societies are usually divided into Independent, First, and Progressive. Others are known as Young Men's, although some members are fifty years old. This might best be explained by the fact that at the time of their founding their membership consisted of young men between the ages of 18 and 25. A visitor to these Young Men's, upon beholding so many graybeards, is bound to observe the paradox.

The older generation arrived in this country with strong religious feelings. Their first concern was to set up places of worship—ansheys. The generation that followed, consisting in the main of young men fleeing compulsory military service, poverty, persecution, or political oppression, organized societies of a more secular nature.[10]

To the query, "Under what circumstances was your society founded?" a number of secretaries made the following replies:

1. Our men, having left their wives or sweethearts in the old country and being beset by loneliness in the new country, assembled at the home of a married landsman. There they would drink tea, play cards, and listen to reports of conditions prevailing back home.
2. A landsman was threatened with deportation because of illness. This led his landsleit to recognize the need of organizing for purposes of mutual aid in times of distress.
3. A landsman suddenly died in a factory. Mistaken for a Greek, he was buried in potter's field. His landsleit learned of it in time. They had his body disinterred, and laid to rest according to Jewish ritual. They decided then to have their own organization with their own cemetery plot.

In a number of the questionnaires the following was a typical account of the founding of the society: "The town after which the society was named had been wiped out completely (war, fire) so it was decided to aid the neighboring towns."

Some societies came into existence not merely because of an immediate need, such as the death of a landsman or loneliness of members, but solely because of idealistic aspirations. The Tshekhonovtser Society, for instance, took upon itself to set up a farm colony in New York State. Having been forbidden to settle on Russian land under the Czarist regime, they wished to do so as a group in this country. They then formed a subsidiary organization, the Home Land Society, and set out to find a suitable location when the whole plan came to grief.

Owing to the curious composition of the societies, serious friction was inevitable among members of different viewpoints. Orthodoxists clashed with freethinkers, traditionalists with assimilationists, conservatives with progressives. The result was dissension and the founding of rival organizations.

In a sense the societies served as a training camp for communal leadership.[11] The more progressive members helped to build the trade-union movement, organize the vernacular press, and found the various fraternal orders. Men and women who are prominent in all walks of life today had their start in such societies. Many of them are still affiliated with these organizations, not so much for the benefits they receive as for sentimental association with their old friends.

Ladies' Societies

Using the ansheys and later societies as patterns, the women set up organizations of their own or as auxiliaries to those of their menfolk. These are usually known as the Independent Ladies' Aid Society, or Ladies' Auxiliary, and symbolize the progress made by the Jewish woman.

Seventy-one Ladies' Aid Societies and 286 Ladies' Auxiliaries were interviewed. The oldest society was founded in 1895 and the youngest in 1935. The Ladies' Aid Society, patently independent, has its own rules, by-laws, and benefit system; the Ladies' Auxiliary is merely an adjunct of the parent organization. A curious phenomenon associated with the majority of the ladies' societies is that to this day their presidents and secretaries are men. Their meeting locale is usually the same as that of the menfolk.

The male secretary of the Mezritsher Ladies' Aid Society has this to say by way of an introduction to the society's constitution:

> We now look upon our society as a big, growing organization. We are certain that our Mezritcher Ladies' Aid Society will exist forever and for all time. The past has taught us to honor and respect our society because of the many good works we have accomplished. Therefore, we look upon it as a sacred duty to uphold the by-laws of this society.

The Landsmanshaft Branches of the Orders

The rise and growth of the Jewish fraternal orders are results of their ability to absorb the small societies without destroying their autonomy.

For some time the question before the various fraternal orders has been whether to let the societies remain landsmanshaft branches, that is, base membership on local residence instead of place of origin in the Old World. While logic is on the side of the latter, sentiment favors the former.

In the annual report for 1930 of the Independent Order Brith Abraham, which was, in effect, founded through the efforts of the landsmanshaft societies, 75 of the lodges listed bore landsmanshaft names.[12]

Much discussion goes on within the orders as to what part the women should play in the life of their constituent branches. The importance of recruiting them in auxiliary clubs is widely recognized.

Family Circles

The latest form of landsmanshaftn are the organizations of kinsmen known as family circles. It proved difficult to determine the precise number of Jewish family circles in New York because of the tendency of many of them to hold meetings in private homes and at irregular intervals. The larger and the more firmly organized circles meet at a designated time and place. Information was obtained on 112 family circles.

In principle, the objectives of most of the family circles are similar to those obtaining in the independent societies, namely, provision of sick benefits, burial plots, and aid for the indigent here and abroad.[13]

The Nazi persecutions of Jews have placed a new responsibility on the family circles, that of aiding their relatives to emigrate from central and eastern Europe. This leads them to seek the assistance of central organizations, such as the HIAS, Joint, and the various landsmanshaft federations.

Namesake Societies

These are societies named for an illustrious founder or member. There are ansheys bearing the name of some revered rabbi, societies named for a worthy townsman, and fraternal branches called after outstanding revolutionary or literary figures.

Forty-five namesake societies boast of a combined membership of 7,482 individuals, of whom 1,762 are native-born.

Relief Organizations

In times of mass disaster—war, pogroms, and persecutions—the landsmanshaftn jointly aid their native towns. Even independent relief committees have been founded for this purpose, especially during and after the World War.

Another and more recent type of relief activity has been in the form of united relief committees and the patronati (organizations whose sole task is to aid political prisoners in Poland). Information was gathered on 39 such relief committees, formed between 1913 and 1938, and 25 patronati.

Membership of the Landsmanshaftn And Percentage of Non-Landslayt

Eighteen hundred and forty landsmanshaftn of all types (ansheys, societies, order branches, family circles, and relief committees) have an aggregate membership of 256,924, or an average of 140 members per organization. On the basis of this average, the total membership in the 423 organizations for which we were unable to secure any figures would be approximately 60,000. Since there are about 3,000 landsmanshaftn with an enrolled membership of approximately half a million, we may assume that one out of every four Jews living in New York belongs to a landsmanshaft organization of one type or another.

The very oldest landsmanshaft is the Dutch, founded in 1859. The first Polish landsmanshaft came to life in 1870; at present its membership totals 180. The youngest society was established in 1937, with 15 members; in 1938 it had 75 members, 71 of whom were native-born.

Most of the landsmanshaftn were organized between 1903 and 1909. Notwithstanding the curtailment of immigration, 32 landsmanshaft societies came into being within the last decade. The situation among the ansheys is somewhat different. From 1928 to 1938 only six new ansheys were founded. The first family circle came into existence in 1887.

Our tabulation covering the economic status of the landsmanshaft members indicates that 75 percent of the total membership consists of wage earners, 15 percent of merchants, and 10 percent of professionals. It was not possible to determine more accurately the specific occupations of the members because the secretaries of the organizations keep no such records. Only in recently published bulletins of some of the more Americanized societies has there been a tendency to include statistical data. Thus, in the March, 1938, issue of the *Progressor,* the English-Jewish bulletin of the Broder Young Men's Benevolent and Educational Alliance, it is stated that out of 104 members seventy-five were born in Poland, twenty-one in the United States, four in Russia, two in Rumania, one in Germany, and one in Austria. The members have a total of 151 children. Eighty-four percent of the members are American citizens. Forty-seven members were born in Brody (Poland).

A number of secretaries stated that when their respective society was founded, many years ago, the majority of the members worked in one specific trade. This was explained by the fact that when a townsman arrived, fellow townsmen procured employment for him in the shop where they were employed. Thus, according to one secretary, his society consisted solely of vest makers. To this day there are many Marmorisher (former inhabitants of the town of Marmorish) in the necktie industry.

Even closer economic bonds exist among members of the family circles. If the leader of one is successful in, let us say, the garage business, his fellow members are inclined to follow the same line.

Every landsmanshaft has a portion of non-landslayt as members. We find Lithuanians in Galician societies, Poles in Russian organizations, and vice versa. Reasons for this apparent paradox vary. A Russian Jew marries a Galician girl; his father-in-law takes him into his landsmanshaft; or a shop worker from one region introduces as a member in his society another hailing from a different region; or a neighbor induces another to join for business considerations. All told, there appears to be an average of 30% non-landslayt in all types of landsmanshaftn.

The greatest enemy of all benefit organizations seems to be old age. Most of the landsmanshaft organizations were originally founded as Young Men's groups, but today, when the twenty-fifth or thirty-fifth or even the fiftieth anniversary of the society's existence is being celebrated, the dangers connected with old age hang menacingly over it. The mortality rate increases. Often the charter member can barely pay his dues. He is poor and sick, and no longer able to work. True, the societies have established various funds for the protection of their members: loan funds, welfare funds, and, above all, funds with which to pay the dues of aged members but these hardly solve the problems of survival facing the societies.

The dispensation of old-age funds follows more or less a uniform pattern in most societies. When a member has belonged to a society for twenty years and at the end of that period he finds that he is no longer able to pay his dues, he is entitled to avail himself of the old-age fund for payment of his bills without forfeiting any of his benefits.

In view of the foregoing, one of the chief problems of the societies consists of attracting young blood into the aging organizations.

Youth and Americanization

An interesting sight to observe at the landsmanshaft meeting is the presence of three generations. There one may see a patriarchal Jew sitting tranquilly in a skullcap. In all probability he is one of the society's founders. At various times he has probably held most of the offices the society has had to offer, and calls everybody by his first name. His word is respected by all. Now the burden of running the society rests upon men in the early forties, the second generation. They are not among the organization's charter members, but owe their appointment to ability and the application of American methods more than anything else. Should the need arise they can conduct meetings in English as well as in Yiddish.

Out of 256,924 members making up 1,840 societies, 38,441, (or 15 percent) are American-born. These are distributed as follows:

American-born

5,214	(or 12%)	out of 42,416 members of religious congregations (ansheys);
17,695	(or 15%)	out of 114,360 members of independent societies;
1,862	(or 6%)	out of 29,872 members of the Workmen's Circle;
1,065	(or 9%)	out of 11,761 members affiliated with the International Workers Order;
120	(or 9%)	out of 1,267 connected with the National Workers Alliance;
690	(or 16%)	out of 4,240 belonging to other lodges;
3,821	(or 49%)	out of 7,734 members belonging to family circles;
594	(or 10%)	out of 6,101 members in the ladies' aid societies;
2,689	(or 12%)	out of 22,496 members of various auxiliaries.

Secretaries of landsmanshaftn are vague as to the ratio of youth members among them. These range anywhere between five and ten percent of the total membership.

Tradition plays a significant part in motivating American-born youths to join the landsmanshaftn. When the father has made a name for himself in the society it is natural for the son to want to emulate him. Others are induced by friends and relatives to join for business and professional reasons. Still others are attracted by the benefits a society has to offer.

Three generations of members attending the same meeting naturally do not find their interests coinciding. Various problems arise, among which the question of language is often a disturbing one.

The Problem of Language

In the past societies conducted their meetings in the Judeo-German dialect. Following is a typical constitutional clause covering this point:

All proceedings and the bookkeeping of this society shall be conducted in the Yiddish language. However, members may use either German or English for purposes of debate. (Constitution of the Brisker Bnai Brith Sick and Benevolent Society, adopted March 12, 1921).[14]

The constitution of the Kolomeyer Friends Association provides that "all proceedings and protocols shall be recorded in the Yiddish language. Officials, however, may use English if they find it to better advantage."[15]

The Yiddish language is generally accepted by the religious groups (an-sheys) as the medium for official business, except for the books which may be kept in English. Article II of the Kletzker Sick Benevolent Society's constitution provides that "reports, minutes, and notes may be written either in Yiddish or English. The meetings, however, should be conducted in Yiddish only."

At a typical landsmanshaft meeting one may hear a Babel of tongues. The old generation speaks a rich Yiddish interspersed with Hebrew phrases and Talmudic proverbs; the second generation delivers itself of a melange of Yiddish and English, and the new generation speaks a fluent English, using occasional Yiddish sayings the way the patriarchal grandfather interpolates Hebrew sayings.

Seventy-six percent of all societies record their minutes in Yiddish. Ninety-six percent of the branches of the fraternal orders prepare their material in the vernacular. Of the lodges, seventy percent write their minutes in Yiddish, fifteen percent in English, and the rest in German. Obviously there is full tolerance for all languages. The linguistic question is intimately related to the cultural problem.

Cultural Activities

To the query: "Do you carry on cultural activities?" 898 replied in the affirmative and 904 in the negative. Distributed according to organizations, we discover that:

273	independent societies responded in the affirmative, 410 in the negative.
167	ladies' societies answered in the affirmative, 192 in the negative.
287	fraternal workers' orders replied in the affirmative, 26 in the negative.
3	lodges answered in the affirmative, 17 in the negative.

43	family circles said yes, 72 no.
36	relief committees answered yes, 30 no.

Most of the ansheys and independents have no lectures on political or social questions. In the ansheys the rabbi delivers a sermon or a guest speaker is invited to discuss Zionism. In the independents the society doctor lectures from time to time on health topics. The fraternal branches, on the other hand, tend to have a specific political outlook and lay emphasis on cultural activities.

Time marches on, and in a number of societies there are discussions as to whether or not to invite a guest speaker of a specific political trend of thought. A number of societies boast that they are receptive to all political views.

Almost every landsmanshaft runs theater benefits. The proceeds derived from the sale of theater tickets are one of the society's chief sources of revenue. The Jewish theater of New York is largely supported and maintained by the benefits conducted by the societies. That explains why most of the plays produced on Second Avenue are practically landsmanshaft pieces. The play begins on the other side of the ocean; the heroes are "greenhorns" who become Americanized. Act I takes place in the small home town, the remaining acts on the East Side or on Riverside Drive. Of recent years this has been somewhat reversed: the first act portrays the Americanized Jew returning to his native town.

The selection of a theater has of late been the subject of heated debates in the societies. The more Americanized members would like to select a Broadway house playing in English. The older generation does not wish to desert Second Avenue. But experience has shown that plays in English produce less revenue than do plays in Yiddish. The societies as a whole prefer the Yiddish theater, but many would like to have it on Broadway.

Aside from benefit performances, the souvenir journals published by some of the landsmanshaftn on jubilee occasions add considerably to their income. The ads bring in many hundreds of dollars. Of late many societies have published souvenir journals which are *de luxe* in paper, type, and binding. To societies whose presidents are prominent manufacturers or businessmen, the journal invariably brings in a profit of several thousand dollars. The souvenir journal issued by the Lipkaner Bessaraber is an outstanding example. It carries ads of the largest fur firms in New York. This can be explained by the fact that the president of the society is prominent in that industry.

The language problem is evident also in the "souvenir journals." Even here tolerance reigns, though in most of the journals Yiddish seems to predominate. Exceptions are the "souvenir journals" published by the family circles; these are printed in English (yet the best journal of its kind in our possession, issued by the Pam-Flicker Family Circle, is printed entirely in Yiddish). Family circles also issue four- to eight-page bulletins at regular or irregular intervals. The Broder bulletin, the *Progressor,* has appeared regularly for almost ten years. Most of the issues are in the English language.

Aid and Mutual Aid

The backbone of the landsmanshaftn is the aid given to individual members in time of sickness or need, and to families in case of death. The society knows each member personally. In the older societies the members have known each other or each other's families in the homeland. When one member falls upon hard times his fellow members show a personal interest in his plight. They are likely to do more for him than is prescribed by the society's constitution. The aid is given directly, with no red tape or humiliation.

The chief beneficiaries are small tradesmen and wage earners. It is they who are frequently in need of loans and outright grants. The societies having such funds available charge little or no interest. Some allow compensation when a member stays home and suffers a loss of wages because of the required seven days of mourning for a deceased kinsman, such allocations being made from a special shive fund. The old age fund has proved highly beneficial. Another fund is kept in reserve to help families facing eviction. A number of societies also have funds available for tubercular members.

Several societies have established special strike funds. This is an innovation, for the majority of the constitutions are silent on the subject. The Independent Bukarester Benevolent Society, founded in 1901, includes an item in its constitution that prohibits members from being strike breakers, the penalty for violation being expulsion. The same is true of the Kolomeyer and a number of other societies. The Liberer Association provides an unemployment fund. According to the Oshmaner journal, the society aided its striking members during the prolonged clothing strike of 1926 in the amount of $1,500. There are also societies which extend aid to strikers in their home towns abroad.

A number of the landsmanshaftn have helped to found homes for the aged. The First Romaner Sick and Benevolent Society is the founder of the Menorah Home on Bushwick Avenue, Brooklyn. Other societies aim to found their own centers, providing homes for the aged on the premises. The Bialystoker landsmanshaft center, on East Broadway, Manhattan, is the largest of its kind in the United States. Homes for the aged were also founded by the Moliver, the Lemberger, and Warshawer societies. The home of the last mentioned, the Haym Solomon Home for the Aged, is on Second Avenue. One of the founders of the Moliver Society is an inmate in his organization's Home for the Aged.[16]

Every society also does much for other needy institutions in New York and throughout the country. Among the foremost is the HIAS; others are the various sanatoria, the day nurseries, yeshivas, Talmud Torahs, the American

Jewish Congress, the Anti-Nazi League, the United Palestine Appeal and others. All of these find a warm response in the landsmanshaftn. As was stated by one of their secretaries, "No one leaves our organization empty handed."

Non-Jewish institutions are likewise aided. From time to time newspaper columns list the landsmanshaftn as contributors of funds for the relief of victims of local or nationwide catastrophes. During one of the recent floods the Ushitser (founded in 1900) contributed money to the Red Cross.[17]

But the chief activity of the landsmanshaftn is to render aid to their native towns, a task beyond appraisal. Of late years, when thousands of Jewish families in Europe have been brought to the verge of economic ruin, the aid of the landsmanshaftn has been particularly timely. Thanks to the work of the special relief committees, corporations have been formed whose objective is not merely to aid the victims with money, but rehabilitate them on a sound economic basis. A significant part is taken by the Joint Distribution Committee through its organization of a landsmanshaft division; also helpful are the Federation of Polish Jews and the ORT, which utilizes American funds to establish trade schools and reorientate constructively the Jewish economy abroad.

Aside from aiding the native town collectively, the landsmanshaftn also render individual assistance, this being particularly true of the older societies. Institutions on the other side—children's schools, Talmud Torahs, community kitchens, hospitals, and homes for the aged—are supported by them. The forwarding of funds for Passover has become a standing tradition with the societies. Distribution of the moneys sometimes leads to differences within the societies, for the more progressively minded members are averse to supporting the religious institutions of their native town without equal aid to the secular organizations. If a Talmud Torah is to be helped, the Jewish library of the town should likewise be provided for. However, no serious division within a society as a result of such a dispute has as yet occurred.

The following figures summarize the amount of assistance rendered by the landsmanshaftn to domestic and foreign institutions:

During the post-war period 1,251 landsmanshaftn of all types raised a total of $7,248,988 to aid the unfortunate in the old country. In 1937, 1,004 landsmanshaftn donated $108,078 to domestic benevolent institutions.

Attempts to Unite the Landsmanshaftn

From time to time attempts are made to unite the independent landsmanshaftn into a federation, but these attempts so far have been unsuccessful. One proponent of such a federation, in 1934, formulated a plan which read in part as follows:

> the associations of landsleit are the only organizations which symbolize a united
> Jewry on a minor scale, because only in a landsmanschaft society does one find

Jews of different political views and economic status . . . seated at one table and discussing problems pertaining to their commonweal. Therefore it is but reasonable to assume that a union of all landsmanschaften in one central body will point to a united Jewry, and that is what a landsmanschaft should stand for. It is the duty of every landsmanschaft organization to join up. (Circular letter addressed to the landsmanschaften by H. Geil, president of the Landsmanschaft Federation of Chicago and Vicinity.)

The plan also suggested the establishment of medical, dental, legal, youth, and child-training departments.

The United Jewish Organizations, founded in New York for the purpose of establishing a federation of the landsmanshaftn, issued a special edition of its journal, *Brotherhood,* on the occasion of its second conference in 1936. This issue was intended to "serve as a teacher and guide to the leaders of the landsmanschaftn and benevolent societies. Various problems of insurance, benefits and incidental benevolent activities will be treated in a professional and scientific manner."

The following are some of the objectives and obligations of the proposed union:

The United Jewish Organizations is a free federation of independent landsmanschaften and benevolent societies for collective activity, not encroaching on the full freedom and self-expression of each individual organization.

The Jewish landsmanschaften have been the pioneers of organized Jewish life in America. Even today they are building an important and vigorous nucleus of organized American Jewry. Notwithstanding, their participation in the mapping and orientation of new forms of Jewish life in America is hardly noticeable.

Among the tasks to be undertaken by the federation were to be:

To study the general and social conditions of the various individual landsmanschaften and benevolent societies.

Help the organizations to inaugurate comprehensive and lively cultural and educational activities.

Help the organizations to initiate activities that are well-adapted to fulfill the needs and desires of the American-born or American-educated youth, so as to win them over to their parents' organizations.

The landsmanshaft federations that exist today (the Federation of Polish Jews, Galician Federations, the Lithuanian, Rumanian, and Hungarian federations) have undergone various transformations. Of these, only the Polish Federation survived its many vicissitudes. The others disintegrated, but were revived.

Time, no doubt, will further develop the course of the landsmanshaft societies and amalgamations.

Forecast

The end of the landsmanshaftn has been predicted innumerable times. Perhaps that is the reason they have been neglected and given scant attention by the Jewish intelligentsia. Perhaps the figures contained in the tables printed here will prove of some value to those desiring to understand Jewish life in the United States. These figures, gathered from original sources, are authentic. They are the result of examinations of records of 2,000-odd organizations, the members of which still take pride in their place of birth.

Good deeds never perish. They may take on new patterns, but their essence remains unaltered. The form of the landsmanshaft organization may change, but its spirit—the spirit of self-help, of concern for the weak, the oppressed, and the needy—will live.[18]

2.

The Social Role of the Landsmanshaftn

A landsmanshaft is literally an association of immigrants from the same country. In modern usage, however, the term is frequently applied to a group originating in a specific city, town, or village. Here we are primarily concerned with the landsmanshaft in the more restricted sense. It is both a product of, and an instrument for, mutual aid, and was created by eastern European Jews who arrived in this country after 1881. They constitute the bulk of the present Jewish population.

Fundamentally, the landsmanshaft is the nucleus from which has evolved, directly and indirectly, the chief social structures of the east European Jews. It has given direct impetus to the formation of a number of large fraternal orders. In addition to the Independent Order Brith Abraham, which had preceded the others, no less than four sprang up within the first three decades of the twentieth century. They are the Workmen's Circle (1900), the National Workers' Alliance (1910), B'rith Sholem (1911), and the International Workers' Order (1930).

The creation of these orders is one of the landsmanshaft's outstanding achievements. When a landsmanshaft joins such an order it usually is allowed to keep its original name, and is given full autonomy. Its basic function (mutual aid) has conditioned its growth and character, and enabled it to become the energizing force within the larger brotherhoods. They, in turn, have raised the operation of mutual aid to the plane of an enormous collective action which serves as guide and model for the unaffiliated landsmanshaft.[1]

Before the eighties, Jews in the United States, being numerically weak, organized societies according to country rather than city or town of origin. In those days they designated their organizations as orders, not as landsmanshaftn.

The oldest Jewish order, the B'nai B'rith, was founded in 1843. It was composed of German Jewish émigrés who desired to elevate their social position to the level of the Spanish, Portuguese and Dutch Jews who held themselves somewhat aloof from the newcomers.

Not a single lodge of the B'nai B'rith bears the name of the region from which the founders came. Instead, the lodges have assumed such Biblical names as Jordan, Hebron, Chananiah, Akiba, Hillel, and Maccabee. None started out with a very large membership. At that time (1848), the entire Jewish population of the United States was estimated at less than fifty thousand,* a fourth of whom resided in New York City. In the main, members of B'nai B'rith were men of means whose motive in organizing was to "alleviate want, comfort the bedridden, give aid and shelter to widows and orphans." Later the B'nai B'rith discontinued life insurance benefits, one of its original stipulations, but it still adheres to its purpose to "defend and protect Jewish victims of persecution."

The B'nai B'rith became international in scope when it founded a lodge in Germany in 1882 and later spread to various parts of Europe, Africa, and Asia. It co-operates with similar institutions engaged in the struggle to uphold Jewish rights everywhere. This activity, which is carried on with dignified restraint, is directed towards reaching and molding popular opinion. It concentrates its energy on combating anti-Semitism and cultivating better relations and understanding between Jews and Gentiles. Thus the German Jews attained the objective formulated by their leaders a century ago. In that respect they surpassed the Sephardic Jews.

The order ranking second in importance, B'rith Abraham, was established by Austrian Jewish émigrés in 1859. Its membership includes also German Jews of the lower income brackets. Its purpose was to grant mutual aid, insurance benefits, sick allowances, and support to the needy.

The lodges of B'rith Abraham designated themselves by the names of their Austrian homeland's royal personalities, such as Kaiser Franz Josef, Kaiser Friedrich, and Crown Prince Rudolf, and such famous Jews as Baron Rothschild, Dr. Herzl, and Dr. Nordau. Some lodges assumed the names of their founders or presidents whom they wished to honor for distinguished service. Later others, out of love for their new country, were named America, Empire State, Harlem, and Manhattan. It was at the height of the Jewish immigration from eastern Europe following the eighties that lodges appeared bearing the names of such cities as Kiev, Suvalk, Ostrolenko, and the like.

The landsmanshaft as an autonomous entity first appeared within the Independent Order B'rith Abraham which replaced the Order B'rith Abraham.

The Independent Order B'rith Abraham was set up by Hungarian Jews. They had the good judgment to make their fraternal order accessible also to east European Jews who joined in great numbers. They called their branches Poltaver, Stanislaver, and Stoliner. Landsmanshaftn named for cities and countries exceed in number those with such abstract titles as Altruist, Fortuna, and Ahovath Achim (brotherly love). In the course of a few decades the membership of the Independent Order B'rith Abraham reached the impressive figure of 200,000, the largest ever attained by any Jewish order.

*Berk, M. A. *History of the Jews up to the Present Time.*

2.

In 1880, on the eve of the great immigration wave, there were in the United States no more than 40,000 Russian and Polish Jews out of a total of 250,000. Was there any landsmanshaft society in existence here prior to that time? A survey conducted by the New York Jewish Community (Kehillah) in 1917 showed that there were 1,016 mutual aid societies of all types, unaffiliated with any order.‡ Of more than half of that number—632—on which data was available, only 9 were founded before 1881.[2]

The investigation carried out in 1938 by the Anglo-Jewish Group of the Federal Writers' Project, embraced nearly 2,000 landsmanshaft societies of all types of an estimated total of 3,000. It revealed that nine could trace their origin to the fifth, sixth and seventh decades of the last century, starting with 1859.

The real upsurge of the landsmanshaftn, as we know them today, started as stated before, with the great immigration wave from eastern Europe. The first shiploads of immigrants arrived in the wake of the pogroms which the Jews suffered in southern Russia in the seventies and early eighties. Others followed the massacres which marked the abortive Russian Revolution in 1905. Recurrent pogroms, notably those which took place in Kishiniev in 1903, and during the Russo-Japanese War in 1904, impelled countless numbers of Jews to seek a haven in America. The peasant uprisings in Rumania, which terminated in bloody excesses against Jews, added their share of refugees. These immigrants blazed the trail for their coreligionists who were later driven overseas by stark poverty. From 1881 to 1936 inclusive, nearly two and a half million (2,416,916) Jews left eastern Europe for these shores.* This number, together with those who were born here, swelled the Jewish population from 250,000 in 1880 to 3,389,000 in 1917, and from 4,228,000 in 1927 to approximately 4,500,000 in 1938. About one half of this number are concentrated in Greater New York.

The Jewish population in New York was augmented from 1881 to 1898 by 533,478; from 1898 to 1907 by 770,036; from 1907 to 1914 by 609,559, reaching 1,500,000 in 1917 and close to two million in 1927. Today the total number of Jews in Greater New York is probably larger.

The Jewish Community survey made in 1917 showed that out of 632 mutual aid societies of all types, 9 were in existence prior to 1881; 205 were formed between 1881 and 1901; 144 between 1902 and 1906; and 251 between 1907 and 1917.**

According to the Anglo-Jewish Writers' Group, which covered 714 landsmanshaft mutual aid societies attached to no particular order, only 2 societies

‡*The Jewish Communal Register for 1917–1918,* published by The Jewish Community (Kehillah), New York, 1918, p. 733.

*Karpf, M. J. *Jewish Community Organization in the United States,* published by Bloch Publishing Co., New York, 1938, p. 31.

**The Jewish Communal Register for 1917–1918,* published by the Jewish Community (Kehillah), New York, 1918, p. 733.

existed before 1881; 167 came into being between 1881 and 1901; 166 between 1902 and 1906; and 244 between 1907 and 1917.

The Writers' survey, dealing in part with the period after 1917, indicates that 103 mutual aid societies sprang up between 1918 and 1927 and only 32 between 1928 and 1937. This drop was clearly effected by the decline in immigration during the two periods caused by the operation of the quota laws of 1921, and the depression of the early thirties.

Should this, then, be taken to mean that the landsmanshaftn are gradually disappearing from the American scene? Not by any means. The survey reveals a definite trend towards their growth and expansion. As against the 88,187 members which *The Communal Register* reported for 632 mutual aid societies, the Writers' Group canvassed 714 landsmanshaft mutual aid societies with an aggregate membership of 114,260. Of the 714 societies, 15 reported a membership smaller than they had at the beginning. Another form of landsmanshaft—the family circle—came to light, with a native-born following of fifty percent or more. Therefore it may be concluded that the life of the landsmanshaftn is not contingent on immigration. Apparently they have other means of retaining their old members while acquiring new recruits.

The testimony of figures gives statistical assurance that in considering the landsmanshaftn we are not dealing with an abstract subject. It enables us to revert to the societies' historical career. Yet statistics are not everything.

The landsmanshaft organization is strictly east European in a qualitative and quantitative sense. Judging it in its qualitative aspect, we are in a position to ascertain the reason why Jews have a proportionately greater number of mutual-aid societies than any other immigrant group. We are afforded a clearer picture of the societies' specific characteristics. With them their real history begins.

A convenient method to study the societies is to separate them into three categories: the synagogic-ceremonial, the nationalistic-radical, and the catastrophical.[3] The first takes in their beginning till about 1905; the second starts from 1900 and runs well into the period of the World War.

Let us proceed with the first class. It was estimated that the 2,500,000 Jews who arrived here between 1881 and 1936* amounted to about one-third of the entire Jewish population of eastern Europe. This assumed the magnitude of a national exodus precedented only in ancient times and in the Middle Ages. We have its tragic counterpart today in Germany and its protectorates. At certain periods in the past it became a common custom for the whole Jewish populace of towns, headed by the chief rabbi and lesser officials, to go outside their city gates and bid welcome to bands of exiles coming to them. They would provide them with food and clothing, and help them start anew. Practices like this help to explain why Jews have been able to overcome all the terrifying misfortunes which have been inflicted upon them.

---

*Karpf, M. J., *Jewish Community Organization in the United States,* published by Bloch Publishing Co., New York, 1938, p. 31.

This tradition of welcoming refugees has become an integral part of the Jewish character. Jews in eastern Europe practiced it when their brothers were reduced to indigence by fire or had escaped from pogroms. During the World War when the Russian high command on the eastern front expelled the Jews living in that region, their coracialists in the interior took care of them. As a result the Jews of one half of Russia were dependent for several years on the other half.

The virtue of hospitality, which thus became an element of Jewish life, is especially adhered to in times of stress and disaster. The poorest Jew would consider himself fortunate if he were able to entertain an impoverished Jew from out of town on the Sabbath. The presence of such a guest in his home would add much to his enjoyment of the holy day.

The custom of extending hospitality to exiles was the impetus that brought about the founding of landsmanshaftn societies in New York. In this case it was primarily solicitude for one's countrymen, then concern for one's own welfare.

In the New World earlier settlers made subsequent arrivals feel at home. First one member of a family—husband, father, son—would emigrate, and later send for the rest of the family. In many cases a distant relative, friend, acquaintance, or merely an interested townsman, would arrange for the passage.

At the present time it is difficult to imagine what an essential part the landsmanshaftn played in the early period of immigration before regular institutions like the HIAS (Hebrew Immigrant Aid Society) were set up to care for the friendless strangers. The former served as first-aid stations of hospitality, as meeting places and family centers. Without them the immigrant might have been helpless indeed. Here were the people he knew back home. They met him at Castle Garden, lightened his first hardships, and found a home and often employment for him. They bridged for him the gap between the Old World and the New. They familiarized him with the elementary principles of Americanism. Under their tutelage he adjusted himself to the new environment.

3.

Hospitality, among other time-honored Old World customs, underwent a tremendous revival in this country. There had to be someone to receive the immigrant. Usually it was the one who procured for him the steamship ticket. Similarly when a dozen, fifty, or a hundred Jews would emigrate from a pogromized or otherwise afflicted town, there had to be someone to facilitate their landing on these shores. Often this aid was furnished by a khevre (religious society) which later developed into a landsmanshaft. Most orthodox Jewish groups maintained (they still do) such societies within their congregations. Their custom of saying the daily prayers with a required quorum of ten worshippers stimulated the organizational process. The only opportunity one had prior to 1880 to meet one's countrymen was at the synagogue. In the early days, devotional exercises took place at the home of a member. But as the group increased, a small hall would be hired and an ark installed. The stranger, witnessing the gratifyingly familiar religious service, no longer felt himself alone in an unknown land.

The synagogue represents the spiritual force behind many established practices of charity. Chief among them are giving outright money grants, or lending money without interest, comforting the bedridden, providing medical care, and in cases of death, keeping vigil all night with the family mourners. An organic part of a religious congregation is the khevre kedishe (the committee that performs the interment rites for a deceased member).

The only difference is that in his native town a poor man received such services gratis, whereas here he pays for them in advance in the form of dues.

From the concept of charity was evolved the idea of mutual aid and various forms of benefactions, which the recipient regarded not as a favor but as his rightful due. As a result, his self-respect suffered no diminution. In time the benefit system was greatly improved, and deeds of benevolence became more numerous. Moreover, since members were required to pay funeral and burial expenses during their lifetime, the societies were in a position to acquire their own cemetery plots, thus reducing the cost. Each member's share of the sick and death benefits was determined in advance. This was a boon to the widow of a departed member. Instead of the few rubles which compassionate neighbors might collect for a bereaved woman "on the other side," here she received 200 dollars outright from the society. Thus she and her dependents would not be altogether destitute. The two hundred dollars death compensation was in line with the custom established by the German-Jewish lodges of the Order Brith Abraham, who in turn copied it from the American type of benevolent society. The last named had inherited it from the friendly societies of old England.

While the transition of the synagogue society into a benevolent one went on apace, there remained those societies whose major concern was the house of worship and the cemetery, and still others who upheld the synagogue without being directly dependent on it. The latter also accepted members who were in no way associated with the synagogue. It adopted rigid statutes regulating dues collections, benefit payments, and all kinds of assessments.

Prior to 1881 the ansheys (landsmanshaft congregations) were not numerous. Afterwards they sprang up like mushrooms after a rain, and just as quickly disappeared.

The oldest and largest places of worship in New York were founded by ansheys. Those who could not afford to build their own synagogue rented space in a meeting hall, furnished it with an ark, and drew great crowds of worshippers on the high holidays.

It is clear that the landsmanshaft benefit society is an offshoot of the synagogue, and its benefit system colored by religious tradition. In changing to mutual aid, its religious nature was not lost.[4] A landsmanshaft readily lends support to non-members. This was particularly evident during the

World War when a society's relief program on behalf of European towns—whole Jewish communities—far outstripped its own here at home. Non-orthodox, socially conscious groups were especially active in this field. Generosity, the feeling of solidarity with unfortunate kinsmen everywhere, is a fundamental characteristic of the landsmanshaftn.

4.

After the landsmanshaftn had provided for their own spiritual and worldly needs, they established themselves on a permanent basis of mutual aid. They no longer needed the guidance of the synagogue. The new arrivals displayed little religious devotion. Once the pattern had crystallized, other lands-manshaftn were formed to cope with the altered conditions. From that moment they became a definite social force and influence in Jewish corporate life.

Their paramount task was to co-operate in all types of constructive action. They stimulated the development of the orders—the old and staid Brith Abraham, and the younger, more democratic Independent Brith Abraham. They extended the life of the former from thirty to forty years; they helped the latter to become one of the largest Jewish orders.

Why does a landsmanshaft join an order? In the main there are two reasons: material and spiritual; the other is to alleviate want and to provide recreation. Materially the benefit system, the mainspring of its existence, impels it in the direction of the order. The order's $500 insurance policy is sounder than the $200 offered by the landsmanshaft. Spiritually, it is in a position to provide a more diversified cultural and recreational program of activities than the smaller independent societies. Furthermore, the very size and prestige of the order helps the affiliated society to expand its own membership. True, dues are much higher: twelve dollars a year in the older order and fifteen dollars in the younger, as against four, five and six dollars a year stipulated by the isolated landsmanshaftn. However, their members soon discover that the small cost comes to much more in the long run. At the outset it appears simple: one pays ten cents or fifteen cents dues each week. But as time goes on the payments gradually increase until at the end of fifteen or twenty years the amount is doubled or trebled.

Many landsmanshaftn have begun to show signs of senility, the inevitable result of their unsound economy. Insurance actuaries have repeatedly warned against its evils, and State laws have tried to regulate it. To many of their leaders the old system of levying assessments appears just and sanctioned by time. It is based on the principle that "all Jews are brothers," and gives young and old the feeling that they are members of one big family, equal owners of the accrued assets. Dues are paid, as it were, "from hand to mouth." Expenses are determined by income. In like manner the amount of the assessments is governed by the cost of sick benefits, life insurance, and administration, without taking into account the proved accuracy of tables on which insurance companies and modern fraternal orders base their rates.

Such a system of assessments, though ill-advised, served well at the outset. Most of the members were young and strong, and less subject to ailments and death. There was a surplus of income over expenditures. But now the situation has changed about. Expenses exceed income and the budget, in many cases, is unbalanced. The younger members, disinclined to shoulder the burden of their elders, drop out. Few come in to take their place. Those who do stay on struggle along as best they can. In the end their families may derive little or no benefit from the money they have paid into the society's treasury because by that time it is likely to be near a state of bankruptcy.

This situation should be familiar to all societies today. Nevertheless they manage to survive despite their methods of financing without benefit of actuarial tables. The First Bolekhover Sick Benevolent Association—Bolekhov is a town in eastern Galicia, Poland—was founded in 1898 by about twenty-five youthful immigrants each of whom had paid dues at the rate of 10 cents a week. Today the society's membership totals 350. It pays $350 in death benefit, seven dollars a week in sick compensation for a maximum of ten weeks, and has its own burial plot. It is a fraternal order in miniature. The Kolomeyer Friends Association was set up in 1904 by thirty-five members. Today it boasts 450 members. It allows nine dollars a week to bedridden members for a period of fifteen weeks and $500 in death insurance. This association also maintains an old-age pension fund.

Landsmanshaft societies maintain their existence by various devices. They employ salesmanship of two kinds. One, which is perhaps open to criticism, is to ballyhoo membership campaigns laden with promises which even at best cannot be kept. The second consists of energetic social activities carried on in order to attract the younger generation. The two societies mentioned above elect the latter course.

5.

Once the stream of emigration had broken the dam, it uprooted large sections of European populations without discrimination. Many of the Jews who arrived here belonged to the "raw element." Of lowly families, and being poor and unschooled, they were shown little or no respect in the old country. In fact, they were regarded as a distinctly inferior caste. Nevertheless they were brawny, wholesome fellows. In this country, where personal initiative is more of an asset than ancestral distinction, these "raw elements" found ample opportunity to work their way up and become esteemed citizens. They learned how to read and write Yiddish and speak a corrupt English. Upon reaching middle age they aspired to those honors and amenities which had been denied them in the Old World. Could the synagogue satisfy their hunger for recognition? Its slights were still too fresh in their minds for them to believe so.

The society, on the other hand, proved generous in giving honors. It bestowed upon its chairman the privilege to call himself president, to decorate himself with epaulettes, shoulder-stripes, and a medieval military hat adorned with feathers. It also permitted him to make "appointments" and distribute "titles."

The old orders, composed of German and partly German Jews who were quite oriented in America, appeared willing to help "dem grünen Juden vom Osten" to find his place in the New World. Accordingly they introduced him to their secret rituals, ceremonials, and regalia which they had copied from the Elks, Odd Fellows, and Masons. The former "raw elements," having hewn out places for themselves but still craving the recognition they lacked in their earlier years, eagerly embraced this theatricalism. It replaced for them the need of the synagogue. In the old country a poor Jew dared not dream of becoming even a beadle of a synagogue; here he might become president of a society. The gavel could give one a pleasant sense of authority.

The Jewish lodges did not carry on these ritual practices in the open as non-Jewish societies do. They proceeded with the mummery behind closed doors. They placed an "inside" and "outside" guard, invented their own mystic signs and passwords, appointed "marshals," "commanders," "majors" and "captains." The presidents and entire memberships cheerfully played the game. It was an "ersatz" gratification of their craving for richness and color.

For them the lodge was undoubtedly an open door to the social life of the community. As a branch of an order, and as an independent unit, it attracted the businessman, the rising doctor and lawyer who enrolled for professional and personal reasons. Young men who sought a foothold in life, a base for a career, applied for admission. Usually the professional man assisted the president in procedure and etiquette. By means of discreet whispers he also corrected his errors in English in the course of a meeting.

It goes without saying that the lodge was fertile soil for politicians. During political campaigns the Democrat, Republican, Populist, and disguised Socialist considered it a good place for the solicitation of votes. All the lodge expected of each speaker was that in his impassioned oration on Americanism, he would say something in praise of Jews in general, of those he personally knew in particular, and, above all, reserve a few nice words for the honorable Mr. President of the lodge he was addressing.

The language of the lodge underwent a change. In the early days a jargon of Germanic coloration was used out of deference to its founders. In this jargon the first protocols were written; it characterized the first Yiddish newspapers in this country.

The transition in language reflected the changing customs of two generations within the orders. The older Yiddish literature is corded with satirical pieces mocking the crude mannerisms and inept speech of the first landsmanshaft members. The theater, too, contributed its share of caricature. Without doubt there was no lack of material for ridicule. Yet, despite this satire, one serious fact stands out. To a vast number of Jews the lodge symbolized some higher conception, and joining one was considered a step forward in the direction of true Americanism. It taught its members English and parliamentary tactics of which they previously had no idea. Many Jewish leaders and orators, who today play important roles in American Jewish public life, owe some measure of their success to their early training.

Of course it may well be that the lodge merely furnished the arena and the audience; the rest was accomplished by the exigencies of the situation, the historical moment, the vital needs of a generation in flux.

Apart from instructing its members in the issues of Americanism, the lodge also brought home to them a clearer understanding of broad Jewish interests. It is true that some Americanized Jews left their own lodges to join the Elks, Eagles, Odd Fellows, and Masons. In this they were perhaps actuated by a desire to round out their process of Americanization; but in regarding only their own benefit, they neglected their social obligations as Jews. Eventually they returned to the fold, but maintained membership in both organizations.

It is also true that the lodge's interest in the broader aspect of Jewish affairs was negligible. It chiefly revolved around the relief of distress among its members and their families. As for the problems which vitally affected Jews at large, both the lodge and the larger order confined themselves to drawing up various resolutions following impassioned platform speeches made at conventions. Neither followed any comprehensive social program until much later when they sent delegates to national organizations which inaugurated a more intensive social activity.

First came the American Jewish Committee. It was set up in 1906 by wealthy Jews, with Louis Marshall at the head, for the purpose of

> preventing the infraction of the civil and religious rights of Jews, in any part of the world; . . . securing for Jews equality of economic, social and educational opportunity; to alleviate the consequences of persecution and to afford relief from calamities affecting Jews, wherever they may occur; and to compass these ends to administer any relief fund . . . for any of the aforesaid objects. (extract from the charter)

Leaders of the B'nai B'rith were the pioneers in this movement.

Towards the end of the World War the American Jewish Congress emerged with a similar objective. This agency is more democratic in constitution and welcomes to its inner council representatives of the Jewish masses. The Independent Order Brith Abraham operates independently in matters touching on Jewish immigration, but only from time to time.

The middle-class member has brought to the lodge a measure of orderliness and a sense of decorum. Its officials are the self-made businessman, employer, and professional man. But the bulk of its membership is made up of the small employer, the storekeeper, the peddler, the orthodox and semi-orthodox worker.

The cardinal principle of both the lodge and the order is to promote the welfare of their members. But in order to achieve a high degree of cohesion, it needs the added warmth of good neighborliness, if not the strength of a social ideal. The feeling of good fellowship pervades the younger order to a greater extent than in the older. The former is mainly composed of east European landsmanshaftn whose members have known one another since childhood. Even after two or three decades in America, their Old World memories linger on, and every time they get together they cement more firmly the bond of good fellowship.[5]

6.

In order to have done with the synagogic-ceremonial phase in the history of the landsmanshaft societies, we must note here a number of indirect contributing factors. The landsmanshaft quite early in its existence perceived an understanding of those social needs which transcend border lines. While immersed in the ideal of mutual aid, it was ever ready to meet emergencies which involved more than its immediate members.

It was a landsmanshaft—the Ezra lodge of the Order Brith Abraham—which in the 1880's laid the cornerstone of the now widely known HIAS, an agency dedicated to the diverse immigration problems arising in this country and throughout the world. It had its inception when the lodge's representatives came upon a heartbreaking case, that of a Jew newly arrived at Castle Garden. There he contracted some illness and died alone and unnoticed. No one came forward to claim his body or provide an orthodox burial. Thereupon the lodge adopted the policy of caring for friendless and homeless Jewish immigrants on the theory that they are all brothers and countrymen. The first move was to rent a basement to shelter them until employment could be secured. It selected persons especially suited for this work, who subsequently became leaders of the enlarged institution which won the full sympathy and support of east European, as well as American, Jewry. To this day the landsmanshaftn form the chief pillar of the HIAS. At its annual conventions they participate in electing its governing council. This body obtains operating funds from the various societies for the HIAS.

This upsurge of trade unionism among Jewish workers may be traced to the landsmanshaft societies. The relative or fellow townsman who had bought the steamship ticket on time payments for the new arrival, was naturally interested in finding a job for him. Usually he brought him into the same shop where he himself was employed. It was not unusual for the shop owner to be a fellow countryman, too. What later became known as the "sweatshop" was originally nothing more than a factory operated by countrymen for countrymen.

Since the successful operation of any kind of business precludes the spirit of pure fraternalism, the consequences were extremely unpleasant on both sides. The employer argued that he was trying to help his townsmen and they, the ingrates, were making trouble for him by demanding shorter hours and higher wages! Was there anything reasonable that he begrudged them? Was he not a friend of every one of his workers' families? Did he not attend their family festivities? Did he not make them substantial wedding presents? But he would never allow them to cut his throat!

The workers, on the other hand, countered that they could not understand how one of their own kind could be such a slave driver and blood sucker. How could one whom they knew well on "the other side" be a boss over them? In the heat of the conflict they would rise as one man, declare a strike, and proceed to union headquarters. If there was no union, the group would set up one of its own. This created a situation in which unions came and went every other day.

The class struggle allows for no landsmanshaft sympathies. The older Yiddish literature is filled with accounts of the economic strife which divided fellow countrymen into proletarians and bosses. It serves as the central theme in Sholem Asch's novel, *Uncle Moses,* a vivid, deeply psychological portrayal of the two economic classes which were born after considerable labor pains in a single maternal body—the landsmanshaft society![6]

When the unions were weak and lacked money with which to finance their strikes, the landsmanshaftn often supplied it. This was especially true of those organizations which later became parts of the various workers' orders. A clause in their constitutions supports the class struggle and condemns strike breaking. Even independent landsmanshaftn of mixed membership subscribe to it.

Let us take the Kolomeyer Friends Association. Its interests are evenly divided between the socialist movement and an orthodox synagogue. A report published on its twentieth anniversary in 1924 discloses that during the general cloakmakers' strike in 1910, which laid the foundation of the present International Ladies Garment Workers Union, it had paid weekly benefits to its striking members for the duration of the conflict. In 1914 it similarly aided members who were out on a bakers' strike. In both strikes the Kolomeyer Friends Association spent 1,675 dollars, which exceeded the amount it had paid out for other needs covering a five year period. . . . This brings us to the second, the ideological national-radical phase of the landsmanshaft societies.[7]

7.

At the turn of this century the main current of the mutual-aid movement was channeled in the direction of the workers' orders. It should be noted that the landsmanshaft society as such was not their nucleus. It was the ideological benefit society, an organization which coordinated its normal functions with an intense regard for labor's struggles and for the principles of socialism.

Such a benefit society existed in 1892 at 26 Delancey Street on the lower East Side of New York. It was dedicated to socialism as a way of life. This may be put in another way: it tied up the theory of socialism with its material work in order to give the former movement and direction. It laid the groundwork for the Workmen's Circle.

In order fully to understand its growth into the mighty Workmen's Circle, it is necessary to trace the influence which socialism exercised over the Jewish immigrant masses.

Basically, socialism is not a by-product of trade unionism. In the early days trade unionism was hardly strong enough to think about socialist theories. The bulk of the Jewish masses—formerly small shop owners, storekeepers, ruined manufacturers, and persons of undetermined occupation (luftmentshn)—here received their baptism in proletarianization. Here for the first time they came into intimate contact with the factory and the union, and learned the value of organization. Every new strike called forth a new union which survived but a short time. Yet while all these attempts at unionization were of impulsive and haphazard nature, the socialist idea systematically captured more and more adherents. Time and again it inspired repeated efforts at unionization, and served as a basis for formulated trade-union policy.

In looking backward we find that Jewish socialism had concerned itself with matters which had no direct bearing on socialism as such. It facilitated the immigrants' shift from Old World provincialism to American cosmopolitanism, from orthodox traditionalism to an emancipated worldview.

The political and economic power of socialism at the time was of little significance. The needle trades, in which it was more or less intrenched, did not occupy the place in American industry that they do today. But it was of immense value as a factor in systematic Americanization. It had prepared about 100,000 "greenhorns" for American citizenship, using a method which fitted their psychology and situation. Socialism, at the outset, was something abstract, a vague ardor for a dream future. Gradually it assumed a more concrete aspect under the pressure of everyday struggles and needs. It developed a distinctly American and Jewish substance in terms of the social aspirations by which the wage earners are living today. The workers' fraternal orders, which emerged from the ideological benefit society, have helped to convert the socialistic dream future into a tangible, practical reality.

The same process was repeated in 1910 when the Jewish National Workers' Alliance came into existence and, in 1930, when the International Workers' Order was built. All three, they and the Workmen's Circle, now occupy the foremost place in American Jewish life, crowding the older fraternal lodges more and more into the background. Without hesitation it may be stated that it was the ideological landsmanshaft which gave the Jewish people three outstanding social organizations.

Following the establishment of the Workmen's Circle there was a movement among landsmanshaft societies to organize along the line of country federations. As a result there are today Polish, Galician, Rumanian and Hungarian federations.

All have come to recognize the potential power of the landsmanshaft societies when welded together. Every type of Jewish national institution leans heavily on them for support. When in 1909 Dr. Judah Leib Magnes organized in New York the Jewish Community, he stressed the importance of drawing them in. During the time in which the community maintained active contact with them, it showed signs of continuous expansion. But once that contact ceased, it deteriorated into a few special committees devoted to Jewish educational and social research.

The American Jewish Congress, whose aim is to safeguard Jewish rights wherever they are menaced, takes good care to have the counsel of landsmanshaft representatives on its important deliberations. The Federation of Jewish Philanthropic Societies of New York similarly solicits their co-operation, and is well rewarded. The Joint Distribution Committee, a nation-wide agency which for years has successfully collected millions of dollars from American Jews for relief purposes abroad, is effectively supported by more than six hundred landsmanshaftn. Moreover, it endeavors to persuade societies outside its scope to distribute all relief moneys collected for their respective home towns and close relatives through its special facilities; this for purposes of safety, economy, and efficient distribution.

The landsmanshaftn participate in every single relief drive, large and small. Whenever and wherever such funds are urgently needed—whether for a hospital, sanatorium, cultural and religious institutions here and abroad, Jewish colonizations, or for war victims and refugees—the landsmanshaftn are always in the forefront with generous contributions. They serve not merely as a source of supply, but as a force of humanity and idealism. Theirs is a form of giving which refines and ennobles the giver. Thus every fund drive becomes a campaign of enlightenment.

Such a potential power, such a vast sphere of influence as the landsmanshaftn represent, must not be neglected. They exist, multiply, change form, and adapt themselves easily to shifting conditions. Leaving them in an unconsolidated state for many more years may tend to dissipate their power. They must be urged toward the central organization wherein their salvation rests.

3.

The Constitutions of the Landsmanshaftn

Every landsmanshaft has its own printed constitution defining the purposes and procedures of the organization in full detail. The constitution is the book of laws to which every member is subject and which the officials are sworn to uphold in all contingencies.

The constitutions were nearly all adopted in the early years of the landsmanshaftn. As time progressed and as they outgrew their usefulness they were revised in accordance with the wishes of the members.[1]

The constitutions were printed in booklet form, ordinarily from four to six inches in size. The language consisted of old-fashioned Germanized Yiddish, with a correspondingly outmoded spelling. A few were printed in German with Yiddish characters. The importance attached to every word in the constitution can be gauged from the following note to the constitution of the Turov Mutual Aid Society, printed both in Yiddish and in English, which reads: "If there are any divergences between the Yiddish and English versions, constitutional interpretation should follow the Yiddish text."

The constitutions of virtually all the societies are very similar to one another. They merely differ in matters of detail, such as the sum fixed for dues and the amount allowed for sick benefit. However, the constitution of a landsmanshaft differs considerably from that of a congregational society which maintains a synagogue and which is strongly concerned with preserving religious Judaism in all its purity as it was observed in the old home town in Europe. Also different are the constitutions of ladies' aid societies, as these organizations are primarily concerned with rendering assistance to the needy.

Although, on the surface, the text of the constitutions is dry and matter-of-fact, it nevertheless mirrors the life of the immigrant generations of Jews who stubbornly clung to their native customs and traditions and who pitted all their forces against the process of assimilation in the western melting pot. Especially strong was their effort to preserve the Yiddish language. In the landsmanshaft the Yiddish immigrant found a nook to which he could retire from an environment that was alien to him.

The Content of the Constitution

Some of the constitutions devote their first pages to a table of contents, others begin with the text, and still others commence with an oath binding upon each member. Two such oaths printed on the title pages of two constitutions are herewith presented as samples. The following is the oath of the Gorevker Mutual Aid Society:

> I, _____, promise and declare in the presence of officials and brothers of the Gorevker Society that I am ready and willing to join as a brother and to become a faithful member. I pledge myself never to harm one of my lodge-brothers, to follow the constitution in all its rules and to remain true to this Society.

The oath of the Tvies Schor Society reads as follows:

> I, _____, solemnly swear in the presence of all those here foregathered brothers of the Tvies Schor Anshe Zalkiev Society that I will follow all the laws of the Society, that I will not betray the Society and its property, that I will not divulge the business of the Society to the outside world, that I will keep in strict secrecy everything that happens within the society, that I will be devoted to every one of its members. On this I give my sacred word and pledge my honor. Amen.

The table of contents of a typical constitution as, for example, that of the Luberer Mutual Aid Society, reads as follows:
Name, Purpose, and Language
Meetings
Officials
Nomination and Election of Officials
Duties of Officials
Committees and their Duties
Membership Conditions
Rights of Members
Duties of Members and Penalties
Complaints
Medical Aid
Entertainments
Amendments and Changes
Parliamentary Rules
Reserve and Emergency Fund
Endowment Fund
Unemployed Fund

Name and Purpose

All the landsmanshaftn are named for the towns or villages from which the members emigrated to America. Proud of their birthplace and as patriots of the hometown, the members wish to immortalize, as it were, its name. The first by-law of every constitution gives the name of the landsmanshaft, proscribing any change of name and asserting that the organization cannot be dissolved as long as it has seven (with some others it is ten) members.

Each society outlines its purpose in its own individual style. The First Koliser does it in the following fashion: 1) assistance in case of sickness; 2) death benefits for husband and wife; 3) burial expenses and cemetery lot. The First Turover Landsmanshaft states its purpose briefly: "This Society is constituted for the purpose of aiding the sick and needy brothers, paying burial expenses and endowments." Another constitution mentions the payment of shive benefits, still another emphasizes the spiritual development of its members. The constitution of the First Shendishover Galician Association has the following preamble:

> The purpose of this association is to preserve the spirit of brotherhood among all the Schendischover fellow-townsmen and thus demonstrate the unity and peace reigning among the members of the Association. This ideal should also be cultivated among the young generation born in this country, thus implanting in them the consciousness of their lineage and descent.

Meetings

According to the constitutions, meetings are held twice a month, on a specified day of the month. General meetings are called once in three months. Special meetings can be called at the request of the president or of seven members. A quorum is necessary to open the meeting (seven to ten members usually constitute a quorum), and at each meeting all questions are legally open to discussion.[2]

Officials and Elections

The constitutions recognize the election of the following officials:
President
Vice President
Finance Secretary
Recording Secretary
Cashier
Trustees (whose number vary)
Hospitaler
Sergeant at arms
Chairman of khevre kedishe (burial committee)

Some societies provide for other officials, such as the chairman of the loan fund, advisory board, chairman of membership committee, of the executive board and doctors.

Most officials are elected for a period of six months. To be eligible for election, a "brother" must have been a member in good standing for at least six months. Some constitutions stipulate that all officials must be literate, and that only a member who had already held another official post could qualify for president of the society. In some constitutions it is expressly forbidden that father and son or relatives hold office simultaneously. The reason is obvious. Some constitutions limit a president to two consecutive terms, but he can run for office again after six months have elapsed.

The constitutions are extremely precise with regard to the duties of the various officials. The hospitaler must visit every "brother" who is ill in bed and arrange for his medical care. He must visit the invalid once or twice a week and report to the membership on his condition.[3]

The sergeant at arms is the officer appointed to keep order at meetings.

Duties of Members

The member is duty-bound to attend meetings, obey the officials, pay his dues promptly, participate in the committee work to which he is elected or appointed and visit his sick "brothers." He must unconditionally attend the funeral of a deceased fellow member. The constitution of the Pukhovitser devotes a paragraph especially to this condition of membership:

> Every member must attend the funeral of a fellow member or his wife; he must be appropriately dressed and come in time. . . . Every member must walk in the funeral procession in the order prescribed and must not smoke during the services. Non-observance of these rules is punishable with a fine of fifty cents.

The Marriage of a Member

Another paragraph of the same constitution reads: "A single member who is about to marry must notify the society to that effect."

The 13th paragraph of the constitution of the First Koliser Benevolent Association has this to say on the same subject:

> When a member has just married it is his duty to propose his bride for membership. The society is to appoint a committee who are to accompany the bride to a doctor for a physical examination. If the doctor's report is unfavorable, the bride's husband is to be considered single and is not to be entitled to any benefit in the event of his wife's death.

Many constitutions provide for the presentation of wedding gifts to members who are about to be married. The Narevker Mutual Aid Society provides that each member who has been in the society for at least one year should receive a five-dollar gift upon his marriage. The same constitution also stipulates that a committee of seven members are to attend the wedding of a fellow-brother or of his daughter.[4] All constitutions are equally emphatic in expelling from membership anyone who has married a non-Jewess or even one who has not been married according to the laws of the Jewish faith.

New Members

New members must be Jewish between 18 and 40 years of age, physically and mentally in good health, of reputable character, capable of supporting their families, and must be married according to the Jewish faith. A new member must be a resident of this country for at least six months. These are approximately all the qualifications necessary for joining a society. The Kolomeyer constitution, however, stipulates further that saloonkeepers are debarred from membership.

The procedure of joining is usually as follows: A candidate is proposed by a member; he hands in a written application together with a fee and a doctor's certificate; he is visited by a committee which gives its report to the membership, and the latter votes on his admission.

The initiation fee varies according to the age of the new member, the older the member the higher the fee. The Ponevezsher constitution gives the following figures:

```
20 to 24 years of age  ...... $1.50
25 to 29   "    "    "   ...... $2.00
30 to 34   "    "    "   ...... $2.50
35 to 40   "    "    "   ...... $3.50
```

Some societies do not admit members if they are more than forty years of age; others do admit them, but only on payment of a large entrance fee. Some constitutions provide for payments from members in addition to the quarterly dues. The Satanover, for example, asks for a $10 cemetery fee, $1 endowment, and 50 cents for the booklet containing the constitution. It also has the following stipulation:

> A widow or a divorced woman from Satanov, up to the age of 40, may join our Society on the following conditions: (1) She must pay $25 entrance fee; (2) $2 quarterly dues; (3) She is entitled only to a cemetery plot with burial costs.

The Pukhovitser constitution stipulates that only fellow townsmen may join the organization. In the second paragraph of the article on new members it states that only those can qualify who are natives of Pukhovits or have lived not more than twenty-one miles from Pukhovits or who are related by blood or marriage to Pukhovits inhabitants. The same constitution also contains the following article:

> Should the wife of a prospective member be pregnant, he must wait until four weeks after the delivery for the committee to make its second visit to his home and report to the general meeting on his family status.

The board of directors of the Pukhovitser are empowered to admit "restricted members," that is, members who may derive from their membership only those benefits which the directors see fit to extend to them.

The initiation of new members is conducted with an elaborate ritual. This is how the Satanover constitution describes the initiation:

> Candidate, accompanied by his escorts, enters and is introduced to the president who inducts him as follows: "Dear friend, before I grant you the emblem of our Society and pledge you as a brother you must give your word of honor that you consider it your solemn duty to obey all the rules and regulations of our Society and cause no harm, by word or deed, to any of the brothers.
>
> "As you see, our membership button—our emblem—bears the reproduction of a miniature anchor which is a symbol of our unity and our spirit of mutual assistance in the hour of need. Just like an anchor that holds the ship, so does this button hold us together in brotherly solidarity.
>
> "When you come to a meeting, and the door is locked, give this password to the guard inside.
>
> "When you enter the meeting you must greet the president and vice president with your right hand on your left breast, and then take your place beside the members.
>
> "When a motion is taken to a vote, you raise your right hand for or against it, but you cannot vote on both sides of the question, that is, both for and against the motion.
>
> "One rap with the gavel means you; two raps, the officials; three, the Society as a whole.
>
> "You are obligated to attend the meetings and to read the constitution; that will make you a good member."
>
> The president now raps three times with his gavel. "In the name of the Satanover Benevolent Society I now declare the new candidate legally admitted into our organization. Brothers, I introduce to you our new member." Then he raps once and the new member takes his seat.

Not all the societies indulge in such prolonged initiation ceremonies, but they do try to impress the candidate with the solemnity of the occasion, even though the ritual may be shorter and simpler.

Rights of Members

SICK BENEFITS. Every member of good standing in a landsmanshaft, who has belonged to it for six months, is entitled to sick benefit when he is ill and unable to work. The constitutions of the various societies, however, make it a point to stipulate that such benefits should be paid only after a certain amount of money had been accumulated in the treasury; some have this sum fixed at $1,000, others at $500. A member who is a victim of venereal disease cannot claim any benefits. (All constitutions, without exception, contain this point.) The amount of benefit, as well as the number of weeks the incapacitated member may draw it, varies from society to society. Some pay seven dollars, others eight dollars a week.

In some societies, if a member is suffering from a chronic disease, he is supported for one year; in others, for two years. Subsequently he receives aid, but not support. All the constitutions contain a paragraph cautioning against the admission of chronic invalids into the society.

With regard to members who contract tuberculosis (a disease by no means rare among sweatshop workers), the Turover constitution states:

> When a member becomes tubercular he should receive $100 extra besides the $20 a week benefit paid to him for five weeks, regardless of whether he is confined to his home or in an out-of-town sanatorium. If it is necessary to continue supporting him, this should be taken to a vote at a special meeting.

All constitutions direct committees to visit sick members and, if necessary, to designate one member of the committee to spend the night beside the bedside of the stricken member.

MOURNING. Every member of a landsmanshaft who sits shive is entitled to a benefit which usually amounts to seven dollars. This benefit is paid only after a visiting committee has attested the fact that the mourner actually sat out his shive. The constitution of the Horovitsher, for example, states that a member who has been sitting shive out-of-town must submit a notarized affidavit attesting his claim to shive benefits.

NEED. A member who has belonged to the society for six months is entitled to relief benefit in case of need. This usually ranges from five to ten dollars a week. To grant benefits exceeding the maximum sum specified by the society, a special meeting must be called and the request ratified. An article in the Ponevezsher constitution reads that

> a member who admonishes a fellow member for accepting relief benefits which, in his opinion, he was not entitled to, shall be penalized with a fine amounting to one dollar. If he repeats his offence he is to appear before a special tribunal appointed by the society to pass judgment on his offence.[5]

DEATH AND ENDOWMENT. One of the chief motives driving every Jew to join a landsmanshaft is his concern with burial ground for himself and his family.[6] The provision of suitable burial ground is therefore the principal activity of the landsmanshaft organizations.

Every society has its own cemetery plot. All constitutions go into great detail about the rights and duties of members with respect to the burial ground, the funeral and the endowment or insurance money to be paid out to the family of the deceased. All societies finance the cost of the funeral, and usually provide a hearse and two carriages and other minor appurtenances for the funeral procession.

Some societies pay a stated sum to the family of the deceased while others impose a per capita tax (usually one dollar) on their members to pay the endowment. In the case of the death of the wife of a member, the endowment, or per capita tax, is ordinarily only half of that paid in the case of the death of her husband. A wife may remain in the society after her husband's death, but her heirs are not entitled to any endowment. If she marries her status changes.

The articles of the constitutions dealing with death and endowment are extremely detailed, taking in all contingencies. Here are a few paragraphs from the Rozanker constitution relating to this subject:

> When a member's child dies and if the child is under his jurisdiction and is under one year of age, it is entitled to have its body washed and prepared according to orthodox ritual, to a hearse and to free burial in our own cemetery. If the child is above one year of age, it is entitled to the same burial privileges as a child under one year of age, plus a carriage.

> Daughters under their father's jurisdiction are considered as such as long as they are unmarried and under 18 years of age.

> Adopted children have the same status as a member's real children and are entitled to the benefits of the society. Step-children, however, are not to be regarded as his own and the society undertakes no obligation towards them.

> If a woman divorces or is divorced by her husband and she takes the children with her, the children are entitled to burial ground and endowment.

Parliamentary Rules

All constitutions devote much space to parliamentary procedure. They stipulate that the societies transact their business in a democratic fashion, with due regard to the rights of the members. They go into great detail about the rules and regulations of conducting meetings. Some direct the members to consult Cushing's *Manual of Parliamentary Rules* in case of a radical disagreement on interpretations in the matter of procedure.

The Constitutions of the Congregational Landsmanshaftn

Though the constitutions of the congregational societies are in many respects similar to those of the mutual benefit societies, they nevertheless contain some points in which they differ widely from the latter. This is especially true in matters of religious observances and rituals.

The congregational societies are closely bound to the synagogue and consider the preservation of religious customs one of their principal activities. Their constitutions emphasize this fact over and over again. The constitution of the Kokhav Yankev Anshey Kamenits Delita says: "The aim of this association is to maintain a synagogue for daily prayer as well as for Sabbath service, also for study."

Some constitutions not only insist on orthodox procedure but also that it be an exact duplication of east European customs. They also go into detail on the synagogue ritual, rules as to who is to be called upon to read the Torah, the sale of tickets for Rosh Hashone and Yom Kiper. One constitution stipulates: "All tickets for the high holidays must be paid for in advance." The Krasilaver constitution contains this point: "A cantor is not permitted to shave or cut his beard and must not be a Sabbath breaker."

The Vazner constitution contains the following points about bar mitzve:

> Every bar mitzvah boy should submit his application for maftier to the beadle a month prior to his thirteenth birthday; he who applies first is entitled to the maftier. The beadle must keep a strict record of such applications.

The work of the khevre kedishe is held in high regard by orthodox Jews. The constitutions of the congregational societies give much space to the duties and privileges of those members who undertake this work. Some give a special preamble of praise to the labors of this committee. The Ponevezsher constitution contains an epilogue composed by the president, which reads as follows:

> To die, but not to be forgotten; every man endeavors in his own way not to be forgotten, strives to prolong his memory in this world. Our cheverah kadishah not only assumes the responsibility for burying the body according to the laws of Israel but also immortalizes the name of each member by repeating the prayer in memory of the departed soul on the day of yiskor. They do everything in their power to prevent the name of a member from being erased from the memory of the living.

The epilogue ends with

> It is desirable that the young members of our congregation should join the chevrah kadishah in order to fortify this body, for are we not mortal?

4. The Souvenir Journals of the New York Landsmanshaftn

The landsmanshaftn, congregational associations, and similar organizations publish books and journals that commemorate significant dates in their history. These publications form a body of writing that is interesting because of their sociological and historiographical character. They depict various phases of Jewish social life in America as well as in the ghetto towns of eastern Europe. Unfortunately, such publications circulate almost entirely among the members of the societies, and hence are inaccessible to the general reader. Most of them disappear in time or are listed merely as bibliographical rarities.

Our review deals exclusively with the souvenir journals, that is, the smaller publications, sporadic booklets and albums, issued by the independent societies. These usually appear on the anniversary of the founding of a society, which is usually celebrated by means of banquets, balls, and similar festivities.

More than sixty of these publications have been examined.[1] Their text falls into the following classifications:

1. Greetings and congratulations, with or without relevant texts; that is, writing accompanying the names of the persons receiving or extending greetings, with or without accompanying photographs. The greetings are generally in prose, but sometimes in verse.

2. Advertisements. These take up a good portion of space, at times the highest percentage. Together with contents listed under point 1, they form the chief source of income for defraying the expense of printing the souvenir journals.

3. Informative material about the given organizations, their history and circumstances of development, activities, and general remarks. From the sociological standpoint, this is perhaps the most valuable section.

4. Photographs and descriptions of localities in the home town. Streets, fairs, markets, roads, landmarks and landscapes. These are often rendered in a poetic manner, permeated with nostalgia for the old country.

5. Society columns.

6. Eulogistic remarks about important dignitaries and leaders of the organizations.

7. Reminiscences of the home town, which are not merely pictures of

beloved landscapes, but also instructive cultural-historical reviews of the spiritual development of the hometown—ranging from medieval to secular viewpoints.

8. Songs and poems written by members. They are of slight literary value, "written by the secretary's son," or "by his daughter."

9. Journalism. Usually home-baked ideas and speculations. Here is a sample of this type of writing: "The cyclone of the crisis has shaken our doors and windows." Yet at times one finds interesting articles in the journals.

10. Jokes, in prose and verse.

11. Anecdotes, folk humor, aphorisms.

12. Parodies on well-known poems, for instance, on A. Reyzen's "Hulyet, Hulyet."

13. Yiddish-English calendars, marking the Jewish and American holidays.

14. Testimonials for organizational services.

15. Obituaries on deceased members.

16. Financial reports.

17. Statistical tables.

18. Lists of past and present officials.

19. Lists of the founders and builders of the societies, together with special articles devoted to them.

20. General membership lists.

21. Honor lists of "star" members.

22. Photographs of officials.

23. Group photographs. One can usually tell whether the organization is orthodox or not by noting whether the members were photographed with or without their hats.

24. Photographs of institutions that the society is supporting either here or in the home town.

25. Photographs of pupil and teacher groups of Jewish people's schools in the home town. These schools are financed by the organizations.

26. Photographs of youthful revolutionary groups.

27. Cartoons and comic strips.

28. Dance programs (of the anniversary ball).

29. Menus of the souvenir banquets. These menus reflect the economic status of the societies.[2]

30. Editorial remarks and correspondence.

31. Serialized novels. In some of the journals, there being no space for serials, we find the announcement of a serial. ("In the near future the novel 'Lost Loves' by Zalek Verlinky will appear. It describes the town Zoshkov, tracing its history during the course of fifty years up to the World War, as well as the life of Zoshkov Jews in America. Please send in your subscriptions . . .").

32. Contributions from Jewish writers. Professional writers, especially

those hailing from the same hometown, are invited to contribute to the souvenir journals either original material done on assignment for a special occasion or reprints of works already published. Sometimes one finds, but very rarely indeed, a cultural-historical article about the given locality written by an authoritative pen.

The language of the journals is sometimes Yiddish and sometimes English; usually both are used. On the average, however, Yiddish is the predominant language.

Of all the souvenir journals examined, only four were written wholly in English. Seldom does one run across a Hebrew article. The author of one such article was a native-born young woman. The editors of the souvenir journal were very proud of her and wished to show her off. "See what a flower we have in our garden!"

The English in these journals is typical "East Side" English; the Yiddish, too, is of a primitive character, written as if the language had no literary style or orthography.

The journals are often printed in a relatively sumptuous fashion. The paper is thick and glossy, the format resembles that of an album, the jacket is of special paper, the colors are deep and prominent, and the whole product is wrapped in cellophane.

So far only those souvenir journals published by the independent societies have been considered. Now we proceed to those journals published by the landsmanshaftn that are organized as branches of fraternal orders.

Thirty issues of such journals were examined. The main features resemble those of the independent societies; however, there are several notable differences.

Among these are the greetings. As branches of central bodies, the greetings of the chairman and national secretaries of the given fraternal organizations are here printed first, followed by greetings from the national executives, the national school managements, the educational departments, and other branches of the organization. There are also greetings from well-known labor leaders. These journals also publish workers' songs of an international and specifically Jewish nature, as well as the oaths and hymns of the particular fraternal organizations.

The Yiddish in these journals is of a much higher type. The articles are likewise of a much higher literary character. Since the membership of these landsmanshaftn often includes many who were active in liberal movements in Czarist Russia, the reminiscence sections of their magazines are of special interest.

The membership of these branch landsmanshaftn being more sophisticated and more cultured, the longing for the old home in their journals is more tender and more articulate than in the ordinary landsmanshaft societies. Poems, stories, reminiscences, impressions of a tour through the old familiar places in Europe—these are the subjects that fill the pages of the souvenir journals:

Often I would dream of the town of my birth—in noisy New York, on the quiet, mysterious Catskills, in Washington, Boston, Chicago, and Los Angeles; in exotic cities in Japan and China; on the cold Siberian steppes and in the tropical Hawaiian Islands, in Honolulu, Harbin, Vladivostok, and Shanghai, everywhere, wherever fate drove me, I would think of my home town in Lithuania. No land and no city could quench my longings. No beautiful landscapes were as dear to me as the muddy courtyard of the synagogue back home. . . . A birthplace is indelibly impressed on one's memory.

And when the same man, after an absence of thirty-two years, visits his home town, he describes his emotions upon crossing the Polish border in the following manner:

Polish is an alien language to me. Nevertheless as soon as I heard the sounds of that language I felt close to it. The feeling of the fatherland seized me. True, Poland treats its Jews as if they were step-children. But Jews have lived there for centuries and are strongly attached to it. What a pleasant melancholy and painful sweetness possessed me when I saw the Polish landscape. I felt like kissing every bare-foot Polish woman, and embracing every landsman, irrespective of whether he was a Jew or a Gentile.[3]

Sometimes the desire to "immortalize" the old home town is so strong that several groups band together to publish one souvenir journal. Thus, for instance, the Ivyer, the Lider, and the Bobrinitser fellow townsmen, organized in Branch 194 of the Workmen's Circle, published one souvenir journal on the occasion of the 30th anniversary of their branch.

Some of the souvenir journals are named for a street or particular place in the home town. Some of them are small anthologies, full of fictional and semifictional descriptions, reminiscences, and episodes, as well as poems about the old town, its landmarks, and types of inhabitants.

In general, souvenir journals are good source material for studies of the economic, social, and cultural history of the Jewish ghetto towns.

5. The East European Background of the Jewish Family

If it is true that the family is the foundation of the social structure of society, how much more so is it true in the case of the Jewish family? Time and again, during persecutions and expulsions, the whole social structure of a Jewish community would be disrupted. All that remained was the foundation—the family.[1]

Often families would seek refuge away from oppression *en masse*. Or, if that were not feasible, the head of the family would flee to a new land, seeking a haven. But in the new environment, his guiding thought and impulse was to regain the other members of his family and bring them together under more propitious circumstances. There is a classic illustration of this in the history of the large migrations from eastern Europe where the bigotry of the Middle Ages has persisted up to the present time. Today, this is borne out to a large extent in Germany and the various countries of central Europe where the persecutions of the Dark Ages have been revived.

In a new land, the Jewish family is instinctively the first to take root, and on the basis of this family life, the entire Jewish communal structure—religious, philanthropic, and educational—is built up, with a kehile [organized Jewish community] to supervise its varied activities. The community is not built up overnight, but step by step. As a structure, it is not exactly comparable with the huge political and economic edifice of a nation possessing its own land, its own sovereignty, and its own economy. Nevertheless, the apparently weak Jewish social structure has a strong foundation—the Jewish family which has survived inquisitions, pogroms, and expulsions throughout the ages.

Just as much as religion has been the stimulus to the survival of the Jews as a people for thousands of years, so has the family served as a stimulus to the survival of religion. Religion has helped to solidify the bond of kinship to such an extent that the institution of Jewish family life is without parallel in the history of the human race.

The patriarchal Jewish family of the Middle Ages persisted the longest in eastern Europe. This type of family has been described at great length in Jewish literature. As an institution it was more orthodox than the synagogue. In the synagogue one prayed three times a day, but in the home of the family one prayed from dawn until midnight. Religion penetrated almost every routine of life. Every move, every act was accompanied by a solemn ritual of some kind. It was family life, more than the synagogue, that endowed the Jews with a spiritual heritage and an endurance to face and withstand persecution throughout the ages.

Jewish holidays, in particular the weekly Sabbath, worked wonders in the Jewish home. In the synagogue the poor man was obliged to worship at the "west wall," relinquishing the "east wall" for the more affluent members of the congregation. But in his home the most penurious man was the master and ruler of all he surveyed. The Sabbath meal was the weekly feast. The poverty of the moment would be speedily forgotten, and there would come to him a recognition of the spiritual richness of things within that exceeded material prosperity. He would abide by the traditional custom of inviting an *oyrekh oyf shabes* (a guest for the Sabbath), usually a stranger in town or a homeless man, to share his meager Sabbath repast. The mitzve of extending this invitation would satiate him more than the actual meal.[2]

While the Sabbath would serve to strengthen even the poorest of Jews for the economic struggles of the pending week, periodic holidays, such as Rosh Hashone, Passover, etc., would imbue him with even greater spiritual sustenance and courage to carry on despite abject poverty and oppression. This is especially true of the holidays that commemorate historic episodes in which the Jewish people were redeemed and rescued from bondage and annihilation. These are principally family holidays. The main ceremonial of Passover, for example, is the seyder in which father, mother, and children participate. It is held, not in the synagogue, but at the family table. Symbolically, it expresses the hope of redemption from the trials and tribulations of the past and inspires and kindles hope for a new and more glorious future. A child who participates in a seyder becomes definitely more Jewish than by means of circumcision. And a child who sits in a suke, built against the wall of the family house and covered with reed, will never depart spiritually from that temporary abode. He shall, for the remainder of his natural life, share the destiny of the "Wandering Jew" and be interred among his own people.

Khanike, which commemorates the victory of the Maccabeans, and Purim, that of the destruction of Haman the Wicked, are holidays that are hardly observed in the synagogue and do not call for cessation of work. After the usual early morning service the worshipper may hurry off to his place of business and conduct his affairs as on an ordinary weekday. But in the home these holidays serve as the occasion for family festivities and reunions. The main source of jubilance is the sude, the feast to which the entire family is invited. The poorest of Jews assembles his family and offers a blessing over a glass of home-made raisin wine. The invitation is rarely refused by the wealthy members of the family, if there happen to be any, and they reunite in the bond of kinship.

Thus holiday and family are synonymous in the Jewish family. A visiting relative is a harbinger of a holiday and vice versa. Early impressed, the child will carry this sentiment with him until the end of his days. In the same manner that an American child will dream of the Far West, so does the Jewish child dream of a relative in a distant part of the world.

The Jewish religion, more than any other religion, has created numerous private holidays centered upon family events. The birth of a baby boy or a bar mitzve each call for several celebrations. Although the birth of a daughter does not call for any particular festivities, her marriage is an occasion for various family celebrations.

Traditionally, every Jew, both male and female, is duty bound to marry and found a family. To remain unwed is considered ignominious. To produce progeny is a fiat of nature. To have many children is considered a blessing. To the poor man it is his only wealth. In the olden days it was not deemed disgraceful for a poor, but upright father to go begging from door to door for his daughter's dowry. Perhaps one of the most remarkable institutions that has survived from the Middle Ages to this day is the Society to Aid Brides and Orphans. Even in this country this society has been known to exist.

In times of epidemics, cripples, either physical or mental, have been married off, in the belief that the performance of the mitzve of marriage would atone for the sins for which God punishes by means of epidemics.

In order that Jewish children would not be tardy for the mitzve of marriage, nuptials would be arranged at an early age, even before children were old enough to support themselves. Up to about a century ago, children would be joined in marriage even before reaching puberty. Under such an arrangement, it became the duty of the wealthier family of the two to provide sustenance for the daughter-in-law or son-in-law, as the case might be.

Even though children were married young, and often against their wishes, it was believed that the passing of years would draw them together and cement the union no matter how objectionable it might have been to the participants at the outset.[3] Often there would be three generations living under one roof: grandparents, parents, and children. Because of this close association, not even a pogrom or expulsion could tear them asunder, and all would strive to bring about a reunion no matter how widely they were driven apart.

Another characteristic of the east European family was its regard for family jewels which it tenaciously preserved. A people who were ever wandering and subject to sudden expulsion had to be prepared to flee with whatever possessions that could be conveniently carried off. The poorest woman would risk her very life in guarding the family heirlooms.

While jewels were valued highly, Talmudic education was placed on even a higher pedestal. "Toyre iz di beste skhoyre" (Torah is the best commodity) was the theme of lullabies sung by mothers to their infants in the cradle, and from cradle to grave the Jewish family fulfilled the meaning of this proverb. Births, confirmations, marriages—every phase of Jewish life was lived under the banner of Torah veneration. A person whose forefathers were Talmudic scholars, rabbis and the like, was considered of "noble birth." A family tree showing 100 years of Talmudic scholarship would serve as an adequate dowry for a bride.

Even in this country there is a family circle which claims to date its ancestry to Rashi, the great commentator of the Tanakh and Talmud, who lived in the 11th century. The organization spends much money in engaging experts to investigate and verify the genealogy of every prospective member who claims descent from Rashi.[4]

So highly esteemed and venerated was the Torah that a Jew who was only moderately well off would readily provide food and raiment for a son-in-law inclined to study the Talmud. As a dowry he would offer the best part of his house, and, if there were more than one married daughter, he would divide his house into several quarters to accommodate his Talmudic sons-in-law. He would scrape and scurry about, seeking to earn the money with which to support his sons-in-law who would sit and study the Talmud, or pretend to study it, until they tired of it and went to seek their own livelihood. The older Jewish literature abounds in accounts of the son-in-law living on the bounty of his in-laws. The custom persisted even after the child marriage idea became obsolete.

No sacrifice was considered too great to make in behalf of a kinsman who volunteered to become a student and votary of the Talmud. The wife of a Talmudic scholar, if the need arose, would assume the responsibilities of the head of the family in order that her husband might continue with his studies uninterrupted, believing that his devotions to the study of the Torah would assure the entire family of a perfect life in Paradise. She was willing to be a family beast of burden in this world in order to serve as her husband's "footstool" in the next world where he would "sit" among the tsadikim [righteous saints]. Such a wife is known symbolically as Eyshes Khayil [woman of valor], and is the first positive female type in the older Yiddish literature.

The second type depicted in the older Yiddish literature was the poverty-stricken widow, blessed with a son inclined to study the Torah and eventually becoming a rabbi. Her whole life would revolve around this son. In the daytime she would carry heavy sacks of onions or apples to peddle in the market place and at night she would pluck feathers for beds in order to save up enough rubles with which to send her son away to a well-known yeshive. Once he was there, she would send him at brief intervals a packet containing clean shirts, tea, cheeses and various home-made delicacies she knew would please his palate. She would dispatch this by an obliging coachman or acquaintance en route to the yeshive town. (In those days there was no parcel post.) While preparing the packet, she would shed tears of longing mingled with joy at the thought of how thrilled her precious boy would be upon receiving the good things to eat.[5] For those were the days of "Esn Teg" (eating days) when a yeshive student, too poor to pay for his board, depended on the philanthropy of Jewish families residing in the yeshive town to provide him with free meals. Each day he would be the guest of a different family, and in the course of a week he would enjoy the hospitality of as many as seven homes.

The moral discipline of the east European family continued supreme so long as the Jewish youth was confined to the ghetto. Not subject to outside influences, they were content to abide by the tenets of orthodoxy and family traditions. But when Russia adopted capitalism, with its free trade, the ghetto walls began to crumble as young and ambitious youths entered the secular schools, industries, and professions. Once they tasted the freedom of the outer world, they began to fret at the traditional family discipline. Consequently, more than one break took place between the older and younger generation. This became known as the period of Haskole [Jewish Enlightenment] which demanded that freedom of thought rather than religious traditionalism predominate in Jewish life.

A "war to the finish" against Haskole was declared by those adhering to the orthodox tradition. The young dissenters were ostracized, and no one was permitted to come in contact with such an individual who was considered more despicable than a renegade. When a son was caught reading a modern work behind his Gemara, or a daughter was detected reading a novel or carrying on a flirtation, serious friction would result between sire and offspring. If the recalcitrants ran away from their homes the parents would sit shive after them as though they were actually dead.

What happened further to the east European family after it had been split is portrayed and described in Jewish literature. The Haskole published it, first in Hebrew and then in Yiddish. The defects of the patriarchal family were described in detail. The kheyder which inculcated religious fidelity into the young was strongly denounced; the desiccating social aspects of orthodoxy were criticized and satirized and a general diatribe against orthodoxy was launched.

On the other hand, Jewish literature, beginning with Mendele Moykher Sforim, criticized the naiveté of the Haskole school. Not everyone, it claimed, could escape the life of the ghetto with its many restrictions. The problem among the ghetto dwellers, it argued, was not intellectual freedom but just how to provide bread for themselves and family.

In the 1880s and 1890s, the revolutionary movement began to manifest itself among Jewish workers in towns, villages, and hamlets. It was in all respects a true Haskole movement, with a strong social-political character, since the first task of the proponents of the Haskole movement was to wean the worker away from traditional Judaism into more practical ways of thinking.

The young dissenters would publicly break the Sabbath edicts which had been formulated and laid down as inviolable by the generations of the past. The religious world was horrified but it could do nothing to discipline the hundreds and even thousands of Sabbath breakers. A bitter animosity developed between the older and younger generation.

The family split, but it was not exactly torn apart. The grumbling sire and estranged son remained under the same roof. It was only the mother, the brave woman of olden times, who forestalled the break between father and son. Like a protecting angel, with outspread wings, did she stand between father and son, keeping vigil over them and intercepting their altercations. She was not going to let her son or daughter be driven out into the more inimical world to face possible arrest or exile to Siberia or be hanged for treason or some similar alleged offense.

A Jewish mother will follow her son "to the grave." Two such mothers we come across in Sholem Asch's "Three Cities," one a mother of the conventional type, who attempts to climb the walls of a fortress behind which her son is being led to the gallows; and the other mother, of the newer generation, who moves "heaven and earth" to save her son from the scaffold. When he is dead, she takes his place in the Revolution. Her heart, her very life belong to her son in death as in life.

And so . . . the two extremes—the ultra-orthodox on one side and the modernists on the other—[have] continued to dwell under one roof until the advent of the World War with its subsequent Jewish catastrophes.

6.   Jewish Family Circles

When one speaks of family circles one is reminded of old-time playhouses whose gallery, or second balcony, was generally known as the "family circle." The top balcony of the Metropolitan Opera House is still so designated.

While in theatrical terminology the "family circle" is a thing of the past, in Jewish communal life it is assuming increasing importance. Here family circle means an association of kinsmen who have banded together in order to strengthen their family ties and provide outlets for common social interests and cultural needs.

How many Jewish family circles are there in New York? When were they founded? How large is their membership? What are they contributing to Jewish social life? These and similar questions will be dealt with in this study, the first of its kind ever attempted.

The Jewish family circles are in their initial stage of development, and their cornerstone is, so to speak, the cemetery plot. A survey of the lists of societies which Jewish cemetery companies release will reveal that the older the cemetery is the fewer are the numbers of family circles. One such list contains the names of 43 older societies, fraternal orders, and individual families, but only one of a family circle. Another, furnished by a newer cemetery company, contains the names of three family circles out of a total of 40 clients.

We obtained information from 112 family circles.[1] From the data gathered, these may be grouped, according to the time of their founding, as follows:

from 1909 to 1919: 9 family circles.

from 1919 to 1929: 26 family circles.

from 1929 to 1938: 77 family circles.

The motivations which prompted the creation of family circles are the desire of parents to safeguard the family ties with their children, the loneliness which overtakes many a family in later years and the political and economic plight of the Jews in central Europe which stirred their American relatives to unite in large-scale relief action.

Originally the family circles were founded mainly by the heads of immigrant families. Today more than half of their combined membership is composed of native-born American Jews. This is precisely what the founders anticipated—to attract the interest and co-operation of their children, particularly those who are married and heads of families.

The majority of the family circles are largely middle-class, since only one-third of the members are wage earners. To the wage earner who has his trade union, his fraternal lodge, his landsmanshaft society, his own political and cultural activities, the family circle is inconsequential, except in times of dire need.

To the middle-class member, on the other hand, the family circle is a means of social expression. In it he enjoys a measure of prominence; he is in his own sphere; and it is close to his heart. Furthermore, it provides him with his own plot of burial ground where eventually he will be laid to rest among his own people.

Instead of individuals coming to the aid of a needy kinsman, the whole family circle helps. It confines its charity to its own indigent members, not to outsiders as other societies do. Whatever money accrues in the treasury from various sources remains for the sole benefit of the members. Members of a family circle who are financially well off will readily extend a helping hand to their less fortunate brethren, in many cases giving them employment.

The descendants of eminent European families, such as those of rabbis and Hebrew scholars—Jewish "blue blood"—are greatly esteemed within the family circle. Likewise respected is the self-made man, he who rose from penury in the old country to the position of wealth in the New World.

The majority of the family circles have either typewritten or printed constitutions, governing their particular activities. The rest eschew constitutions as a matter of principle, contending that persons related by blood require no written regulations to govern their conduct. Any differences that might arise, they claim, should be straightened out over a cup of tea around the family table and not by ironclad regulations.

Most of the constitutions cover the following points: name of organization, language employed at meetings, admission and expulsion of members, election of officers and their duties, income and expenditure, selection of various committees, rights and duties of members, liquidation of the circle, and agenda.

The constitutions of some of the family circles indulge in even greater strictness in regard to admission of new members and procedure at meetings than do those of the landsmanshaft societies. One such constitution, written by a circle only three years in existence and having some thirty members on its rolls, states in part:

Items pertaining to admission to membership:

1. He must be related by blood to one of the charter members.
2. He must be a Jew.
3. If about to be married, the ceremony must be performed in the orthodox tradition.

Election of officials is to take place in the following manner:

Each member is given a ballot containing the names of the candidates. The member indicates his choice by marking an x next to the name of the candidate he prefers.

The president appoints three inspectors to guard the ballot box. He asks each member to vote. Then the recording secretary calls the roll. As the names of the members are read each in turn drops his marked ballot into the box.

The inspectors count the ballots, and the secretary checks with the number originally handed out. Then the inspectors call out the names of the candidates and the secretary, his assistant, and one of the inspectors record the number of votes polled by each candidate. The inspector then announces the total number of votes received by each candidate, and if this total tallies with that arrived at by the secretary and his assistant he is to call out the name of the winning candidate.

The organization's treasurer is obliged to put up a bond of a specified amount and,

at the expiration of his term of office he must turn over the family circle's funds and property. When the organization's officials are satisfied with the accounting his security is returned to him.

The family circles may be divided into two categories: (1) Organizations that furnish burial service, sick benefits, and loans; (2) Those that merely provide entertainment for their members.

The older an organization is the more solidified and more affluent it is, i.e., in the possession of cemetery lands, bank balances, and the like. The newer circles as a rule are inclined to devote their whole time to the provision of entertainment, but experience has shown that this is not enough to retain the lasting interest of members who in time become more settled and more practical in their outlook, and begin to think seriously of the future.

Of the 112 family circles considered:

52 own burial grounds,

42 extend benefits but own no burial grounds,

18 are dedicated to "having a wonderful time."

The minutes kept by the circles (nearly all are written in longhand) reveal something of their activities. The first ten such reports examined tell of conducting raffles, the purchase of a sweepstake ticket by the president, gifts presented to sick members and to bar-mitzve boys, entertainments arranged by the circle, and thanks to this or that "sister" for having sold so many tickets for a theater party or similar activities.

When the family circle is ready to take title to burial plots or erect a cemetery gate, the report is more detailed. The following is an illustration:

The chairman of the cemetery committee reports that it visited the cemetery and examined the condition of the gate and the inscriptions thereon. In the opinion of the committee members the inscriptions should have been made on the outside of the gate. After a discussion of the matter, it was decided that the official inscription be changed accordingly and that it be in English letters, but that the names of individual members may be inscribed either in Yiddish or English. After a prolonged debate the question was postponed to the next meeting.

The minutes also revealed that among the more important events in the life of family circles are the marriages of the members' children, which are recorded in great detail. The items concerning funerals, though written with feeling, are briefer in nature. When there are no sick lists the reports of the hospitaler are likewise brief, but more cheerful.

Not one of the ten records examined makes any mention of a discussion in regard to social or kindred problems. From conversations with members of various circles, we learned that attempts have been made to direct their interests into broader social channels, but in all cases the more influential members blocked the moves with the argument that the family circle's interests would best be served if it maintained the attitude of "no politics" outside the circle.

Several circles publish elaborate anniversary journals. On the occasion of its twenty-fifth anniversary, the Shiffrin Family Association issued a souvenir book of sizable format. It contained contributions by members in both Yiddish and English. Another book of this type was issued in 1938 by the Pam-Flicker Family Society on the eve of its tenth anniversary. Other circles issue mimeographed bulletins at regular or irregular intervals. A monthly bulletin is published by the Feit-Ulster Family Society.

A number of older societies issue family books, or chronicles. The Michael Tenzer Family Society released a tenth anniversary jubilee book (in English) of more than 200 pages.* It contains a comprehensive record of the family's activities.

From time to time announcements of family circles' celebrations are printed in the Yiddish press. The following, which appeared in the *Jewish Day,* is an example:

> The other Sunday . . . Aunt Sheindel's 75th birthday was celebrated at her home by the Sheinberg Family Aid Society. . . . Among the 90-odd guests were new arrivals from Europe, including her brother whom she had not seen for 38 years. It was a most interesting family reunion. The chairman of the arrangements committee, in the name of the society, presented her with a check for the sum of $75, and promised that if she lived to reach beyond the age of one hundred years the society would present her with $100 for each additional year. The aunt related anecdotes associated with her early life; these deeply moved those assembled.

*Kerstein, Solomon (editor). Jubilee Volume of the Michael Tenzer Family Circle. Tenth Anniversary 1927–1937. New York, 1937.

The publications of the Kramer Family Circle warrant special interest. They are:

1. *The Life of Morris L. Kramer: A Biographical Sketch of a Jewish Scholar and Businessman.* Compiled and arranged by a group of his friends and admirers, New York, 1926. This book contains 400 pages, and is written in both Yiddish and English and deals with the founder of the Kramer Family Circle.
2. *Kramer Family Song Booklet,* 66 pages. This contains a collection of English and Hebrew songs sung by the family circle on Saturday evenings at the home of the widowed mother, to mark the passing of the Sabbath. The circle has also issued special programs containing the names of the selected song leaders as well as the titles of their favorite songs.
3. A compilation of reprinted articles eulogizing and commemorating the departed founder.

The cover of the song book is inscribed in Hebrew gilt letters, as follows: "How good and how pleasant it is for the brethren to dwell together in unity" (Psalm 133). The book opens with the American anthem, "The Star-Spangled Banner," followed by the Hebrew, "Hatikvah." The greater part of the book consists of Yiddish folk songs and songs of Jewish pioneers in Palestine. The text is printed in Latin characters for the benefit of those unable to read Hebrew.

The circle observes Sabbath night with all its traditional color. A collation is prepared for the guests who make merry far into the night. Some of these festivities have been filmed for the benefit of future generations. From time to time they are flashed on a screen to the delight of the assembled members, especially the youth.

On the anniversary of the death of the founder a sum of money is donated in his memory to various yeshives and Talmud Torahs.

The present leader of the Kramer Family Circle is the son of the founder, a successful attorney in his middle forties. His office, on the sixtieth floor of a midtown skyscraper, contains the family archives in which every letter and scrap of paper in his father's handwriting is preserved. An oil portrait of the senior Kramer, who was a disciple of the Lubavitsher Rabbi, decorates the wall; an amulet is fastened on the office door, and a collection box of the Keren Kayemes [Jewish National Fund] is on his desk. Scriptural works mingle with law books. The attorney and his brothers adhere to orthodox traditions.

The 112 family circles may serve as a cross-section of Jewish family life in America, notably of the Jewish middle class, notwithstanding the number of wage earners included in the membership. A spirit of camaraderie prevails at all meetings: the members address each other by their first names, and all, rich or poor, enjoy equal rights.

It was impossible to obtain a total figure with regard to individual family members, since some circles count their membership not in terms of individuals but in family units.

Of the 112 family circles:

     97   have a total membership of 7,925 individuals;

     15   have a total of 786 member-families, the largest comprising 465 individual members, the smallest 15.

Of the individual members:

     52% are native-born;

     85% of the immigrant members are American citizens;

     20% are between the ages of 18 and 30;

     51% are businessmen;

     35% are workers;

     14% are professionals.

Most circles hold monthly meetings, others semi-monthly, a small number once every three months.

One of the larger circles was selected for a detailed study.[2] This circle originated in a Polish town a century ago. At that time there arrived in Bialystok a Jew from the village of Kozshlitsk. Soon he was followed by four young Jews from the same village. Attracted by his pretty daughters, they paid frequent visits to his house. The bond between the families was made firmer by marriage, and was extended by the intermarriage of the offspring. As a result, a brotherhood society was formed, acquiring its own synagogue and holy scroll. In time of need the interrelated members came to one another's aid.

When the young folk emigrated to America they at once tried to set up a family circle to cement their family ties, but did not succeed in their attempt until two decades later. Once organized they proceeded to purchase a cemetery plot—not a holy scroll as was done by their forebears in Bialystok. While the provision of burial ground was a primary function of the family circle, its main purposes were the perpetuation of the family tie, mutual aid, and relief of distressed relatives here and abroad.

Today the family circle is composed of four generations. The eldest is in its seventies and seldom attends meetings or other functions, except weddings, anniversary celebrations, and funerals. The central nerve of the society is the second generation, the children of those who originally founded it in Bialystok. Their ages range between 45 and 50. Many of them have induced their married children to join the society.

The sixty-odd families of the circle include more than 300 individuals. Of the heads of families thirty are wage earners, fifteen small businessmen, four big manufacturers; the rest are professionals or white-collar workers. Three are on WPA work relief.

"I am looking forward to a hundred years hence," the president of the family circle remarked,

    when our grandchildren and great grandchildren will visit the cemetery and see the remains of a family that stood together through thick and thin. This will impress itself on their memory.

The family circle regards youth as a major problem. The young are drifting away from their family ties; they show little or no interest in sick benefits and burial plots. What has the family circle to offer them? Its leaders realize that without them there is no future for their organization. In order to attract the youth, parties and balls are arranged at short intervals.[3]

Not until the young grow older, marry, beget children, and settle down to the more practical affairs of life do they begin to consider the family circle more seriously. Growing responsibilities cause them to think of sick benefits, need for closer family ties, and burial plots.

Among the circle's sixty-odd families there are no cases of divorce or mixed marriage. Though the majority of the members fall short of strict orthodoxy, they will eat no food that fails to conform to the dietary laws (kashrus). Ordinarily they observe the Jewish holidays, and participate in the religious services only on the Jewish New Year and Day of Atonement.

As one examines the lives of Jewish parents and their offspring within the circle, one is inclined to conclude that the immigrants of yesterday are better off economically than their American-born offspring today, notwithstanding the latter's better opportunity to achieve economic security. School and college diplomas alone are evidently not the guarantors of a successful career.

The Jewish family circle, as an institution in this country, is in its early stage. It is not easy to foretell its future course and development. One thing, however, is clear: many forces have given rise to it, and its continued development merits close attention.

7.

Jewish Family Life in New York City

Economic Status[1]

The economic life of the Jewish family is inextricably interwoven with the general economy of the Jewish community which in turn is bound to the general economic structure of the country.

From the study that we have made on family circles, we have gained a clearer perception of the economic status of the Jewish family and its economic handicaps. The story of the families in our circle being similar to the story of tens and hundreds of thousands of other Jewish families which have immigrated to America, may serve as a criterion of the state of the Jewish population in New York City.

The members of our circle immigrated to this country from the well-known Jewish city of Bialystok. They did not all come at once, but in small numbers. At first a father came, then a brother, a sister, or a son. Everyone tried, according to his ability, to bring over his nearest ones as quickly as possible.

Not one member of the old generation was born with a silver spoon in his mouth. Most of them were born in poverty-stricken homes, and at ten and twelve years of age were obliged to become breadwinners. Many learned a trade, such as tailoring, bricklaying, or weaving. Others became coachmen or small traders.

Here in America, as in the case of most immigrants in that period, the newcomers went through hard and bitter times. They toiled long hours in sweatshops for small wages. With the exception of one immigrant who brought with him a goodly sum of money from the old country, all had to start life anew from scratch.

The fact that most of the immigrants of our circle were skilled workers was in their favor. As soon as they debarked they secured employment in their respective trades. Those who were tailors in the old country went to work in tailoring establishments; those who were house builders became bricklayers and artisans. The very first immigrant of the family circle, a cap maker, secured employment in a cap factory the second day after his arrival in this country.

The new economic standard of living caused many of the members to abandon their old occupations and to adapt themselves to new ones. Two such examples are given below, one of an immigrant, and the other of a native-born member.

Example number one: In Bialystok he was a tannery worker. Today at fifty-one he is in the garage business, his earnings averaging $30 to $35 a week. He has a wife and two married children.

It took him thirty years to acquire his present state. As he expressed it, those were thirty years of bitter struggle, drifting from one job to another. He doesn't even recall the number of jobs he had. And those that he does recall tell a tale of human drudgery and exploitation.

First job: Soon after his arrival in America at the age of twenty-one, he became a grocery boy, working six days a week for two dollars. Every day he had to run up and down hundreds of flights of stairs, delivering orders.

Second job: A moving man, lugging heavy pieces of furniture on his back up and down four and five flights of stairs for eight dollars a week.

Third job: Employed in a second-hand furniture store for eight dollars a week.

Fourth job: Spent several hard years in a factory manufacturing iron bedsteads. Earned from seven to nine dollars a week.

Fifth job: Again employed in a second-hand furniture store, this time getting nine dollars a week.

Sixth job: Again a furniture carrier in the moving business—wages eight to nine dollars a week.

Seventh job: Learned to make caps. Several years later became a master cap maker, earning twenty to twenty-five dollars a week. Worked at this trade for several years, saved some money, and finally bought a garage which he owns to this day.

Example number two: He was born in New York. At present he is in the early forties and has a wife and child. He has held the following jobs:

First job: Upon finishing public school, he became a butcher boy at $2.50 a week.

Second job: In a cosmetic factory—long hours, unsanitary conditions, eight dollars a week.

Third job: Shipping clerk, eight dollars a week.

Fourth job: Cutter of women's hats, thirty to thirty-five dollars a week.

Fifth job: A volunteer sailor in the United States Navy during the World War.

Sixth job: Bought a garage which proved unprofitable.

Seventh job: A cap maker.

Eighth job: An insurance agent.

Ninth job: Again a cap maker.

Tenth job: A taxi driver.

Eleventh job: Became a building contractor in partnership with another man and lost his money.

Twelfth job: A blocker of hats.

Thirteenth job: Again a taxi driver.

Fourteenth job: Became a buyer of old gold, in partnership with another man.

And finally he had to apply for relief.

The two examples are characteristic of many of those who belong to the circle. They tell of endless struggle, of vast energy and initiative expended by persons in order to better their lot. They also emphasize the industrious character of our family circle.

According to the study, sixty percent of the members of the family circle, upon arriving in this country, adopted callings that were different from those practiced in the old country. The remaining forty percent continued in the occupations they had had in the old country.

In order to simplify the tabulation of the statistical data gathered, we divided our family circle into several groups. Taking one of the groups, a more typical one containing twenty men and the same number of women, we compared their occupations in the old country with the ones they pursued in this country.

Men

Occupation in the Old Country	Occupation in this Country
Hat maker	Cap maker
Pharmacist	Manufacturer of cosmetics
Coachman	Storekeeper
Two tailors	Two pressers at cloaks
Tailor	Clothing manufacturer
Tailor	Official in the Cloakmaker's Union
Cobbler	Presser of cloaks
Cobbler	Truck driver
Tailor	Garage owner
Roofer	Garage owner
Weaver	Real estate man
Printer	Restaurant owner
Teacher	Cutter of dresses
Leather worker	Buyer in a fur shop
Coachman	Fur worker
Carpenter	Peddler
Shoemaker	Plumber
Two bricklayers	Two bricklayers

Of the twenty women who worked in the old country at weaving, tailoring, or trading, only two became factory workers in this country. The rest married and became housewives.

In the early years some of the married women continued with their outside employment in order to help their husbands establish themselves. One of them, after a hard day's work of cooking, cleaning, and caring for several children, used to slip into her husband's garage in the evening, unobserved by her neighbors, and help her husband wash automobiles until late at night.

Having a more or less clear picture of the occupations of the first generation immigrants, it would be interesting to examine the vocations of their American-born offspring and see how many of them have followed in the footsteps of their parents and how many have adopted occupations that were unknown to their parents in the old country.

The following tabulation was compiled after studying two typical groups in our family circle containing twenty breadwinners each.

Occupations of the Young, American Generation

Men	Women
Policeman	Six housewives
Druggist	Teacher
Garage owner	Designer of shoes
Foreman in a hat factory	Private secretary
Roofer	Two bookkeepers
WPA Worker	Two office girls
Taxi driver	Two stenographers
Furrier	Milliner
Civil Service employee	Dressmaker
Salesman	Saleslady
Cafeteria manager	Worker in a paper-box factory
Lawyer	Teacher
Milkman	
Public accountant	
Builder	
Designer	
Aviation engineer	
Sailor	
Blocker of hats	
Bricklayer	

The men's list contains only two cases in which the American-born youth adopted their father's line of work. One was a foreman in a hat factory, whose father was a hat maker, and the second, a bricklayer's son, who completed his law course some years ago, but to this day is working beside his father as a bricklayer.

Many members of our circle have been associated with the trade-union movement. To this day many belong to cloakmakers', bricklayers', millinery, and furriers' unions.

Just as their fathers did in the old country, so have the American children, often in their earliest youth, taken the responsibility upon themselves to contribute to the scant family income.

From two groups of thirty children each, the first taken from the old generation, the second from the American-born, we see the following:

Began to Work in the Old Country

Boys	Girls
4 at 10 years of age	1 at 10 years of age
4 at 11 " " "	1 at 11 " " "
9 at 12 " " "	5 at 12 " " "
7 at 13 " " "	4 at 13 " " "
1 at 14 " " "	9 at 14 " " "
1 at 15 " " "	2 at 18 " " "
1 at 16 " " "	8 did not work
1 at 17 " " "	
1 at 18 " " "	
1 at 20 " " "	

We will now compare the two tables with the same number of children in America.

Began to Work in America

Boys	Girls
3 at 12 years of age	1 at 13 years of age
3 at 13 " " "	2 at 14 " " "
10 at 14 " " "	5 at 15 " " "
4 at 15 " " "	9 at 16 " " "
5 at 16 " " "	7 at 17 " " "
1 at 17 " " "	4 at 18 " " "
1 at 18 " " "	2 did not work
3 at 20 " " "	

According to these figures, it appears that even in this country children begin to look for work when they are very young. Nevertheless, the children of our circle, as most children in New York City, have been better situated than children in the old country. They have been better fed and better clothed and better educated than their immigrant parents when they were children in the old country.

In the course of years several of the immigrant parents of our circle became manufacturers and real estate operators. Those who failed to acquire substantial incomes made a good, though a hard-earned living. The onset of the crisis of 1929, which brought in its wake economic havoc to millions of families throughout America, also had its effect on our family circle. Workers who previously earned a good wage and lived a quiet, contented life, suddenly began to receive one wage cut after another. A number who had retained good jobs for years or operated a thriving business, suddenly found themselves minus jobs or business of any kind.

The present weekly earnings of the members are as follows:

Number of Families	Weekly Income
3	$100 and upward
6	$60 to $70
20	$40 to $50
15	$30 to $40
10	$20 to $25
5	$15 to $20
1 unemployed	

Since the economic well-being of a family is dependent on the number of its members, it is important to show how big the families are in our circle.

Despite dire poverty, the European family usually contained a large number of children. From information obtained from fifty families, it was found that, not counting the deceased children:

  6 families had 10 to 12 children each
  8 families had 7 to 10 children each
10 families had 5 to l7 children each
12 families had 4 to 5 children each
14 families had 3 to 5 children each

The families in our circle followed the general American tendency of having fewer children. While the parents averaged about seven children per family in the old country, the offspring in this country averaged a little over two children per family.

In studying the housing situation of our members we found that:

18 families own their own homes, mostly in Brooklyn, usually the two-family type, consisting of five or seven rooms
  2 families live in six rooms each
  3 families live in five rooms each
15 families live in four rooms each
24 families live in three rooms each
  6 families live in two rooms each

With regard to rent, the following was noted:

10 families owning their own homes have an average expenditure of from $30 to $40 a month for upkeep, taxes, etc. (exceptions are the two brothers, the cloak manufacturers, who reside in elegant homes)
  7 families pay between $50 and $60 a month rent

14 families pay between $40 and $50 a month rent
16 families pay between $30 and $40 a month rent
 6 families pay between $25 and $30 a month rent
 7 families pay between $15 and $20 a month rent

Twelve families of our circle own their automobiles. About 70 percent of them carry life insurance, the average principal on policies ranging from $1000 to $2000. Because of hard times, the policies of several members in the circle had lapsed. Forty percent have telephones in their homes. Seventy-five percent have mechanical refrigerators. Thirteen percent live in elevator apartments. Eighty percent do their own house cleaning. Two percent have full-time maids. Thirty percent have vacuum cleaners.

The economic status of the families in our circle can be divided into three parts:

At the very top of the ladder we find one successful real estate operator, two brothers who are rich clothing manufacturers, one owner of a cosmetic factory, and several owners of smaller factories—altogether about ten percent of the total. The middle rung of the ladder is occupied by the majority: small tradesmen, owners of garages, and better-paid workers. They account for about seventy percent of the total number of families in the circle. Finally come the tailors, shoemakers, three WPA workers, and one unemployed member of the circle, totaling twenty percent.

The Youth

According to the report on the activities of the youth, only ten percent of the native-born or Americanized youth adopted the occupations of their parents. The majority entered other fields of endeavor. While most of the fathers were employed in the needle trades, garage business, or bricklaying, their American-born or Americanized sons became lawyers, pharmacists, managers of small businesses, furriers, milkmen, and taxi drivers; their daughters became bookkeepers, stenographers, saleswomen, and teachers.

The reports also reveal that a large portion of the youth had to give up their college education owing to the depression. Others who intended to study and prepare for a profession have been forced to stifle their ambitions for the same reason. On the other hand, many with college diplomas are now employed in other vocations than the ones for which they had prepared themselves. Of two young men who are graduate lawyers, one is a bricklayer and the other works in his father's perfume factory as a salesman.

The problem of obtaining employment, the uncertainty of the job, the general hardships blocking the way to success have, in a large measure, disillusioned the youth, and they are merely marking time, hoping that at some future date they will be able to establish themselves in the vocation for which they prepared themselves at school.

One of the reports contained a particularly poignant statement of disillusionment and discontent. A twenty-year-old young man, son of one of the families, whose father is a presser of cloaks, gave vent to the following utterance:

> I studied with great enthusiasm, always receiving high marks. I graduated from public school, high school, and college. My educational status is considered exemplary. Yet I do not know which way to turn. I have been seeking employment for weeks, following the want ad pages closely every day. But it's no use. I am tired of walking the streets. If something does not turn up soon, I shall enlist in the Army. There seems to be no better way out.

The problem of anti-Semitism has complicated the economic chances of the youth. Of late many American-born Jews have been unable to find jobs because of their race. Such a case of economic anti-Semitism was experienced by a daughter of a member of the circle when she applied for a job at a utility company.

The general unemployment on one side and the growing anti-Semitism on the other are reflected in the life of the new generation of our family circle, which may be a criterion of the state of Jewish youth in America.

Cultural Status[2]

"When there is no bread there is no Torah" is an old Hebrew proverb. The truth of this saying is borne out in large measure by facts and figures relating to the cultural status of individual members of our family circle, as garnered from their biographies. Throughout most of their lives they were engaged in a ceaseless struggle for the primal necessities: food, clothing, and shelter. They had little or no opportunity for cultural development.

Take for example a typical member of the older generation. His father was a coachman, barely able to make a living for his wife and six children. The wolf was always at the door.

The mother, in order to supplement the family income, would spend the greater part of the day at the market place, plodding from one stand to another in quest of a bargain which she would then resell at a small profit to the more prosperous Jews of her acquaintance. The father died when the member was ten years old. As a boy he was taken out of the kheyder and apprenticed first to a coachman, then to a builder, and again to a coachman. His education was abruptly cut short and he forgot all about it in the struggle for the few kopeks that his labors driving the coach brought him. Beyond reading the Hebrew prayers and a slight reading and writing of Yiddish, he knew nothing.

Not until he was on his way to this country, when he was about to communicate with his wife, did he realize that he could barely write a letter in his own language. The few words he managed to extract from his pen came with the utmost difficulty.

To say that he was entirely lacking in culture would be inaccurate, even though he was unable to read and write Russian, the national language of the land of his birth. Children of poverty-stricken parents, such as his, did not have the opportunity for a secular education. The traditions of Judaism, the ability to read the Hebrew prayers, and a knowledge of the stories and legends of ancient Jewish times that are handed down from parent to child were his priceless possession. True, his imagination had been fired, and his desire to acquire knowledge was strong, but he was not in a position to satisfy it.

Almost all the members of the older generation, both men and women, deplore their lack of education. At the ages of eight, nine, ten, and twelve they were apprenticed to builders and coachmen, or sent to work in near-by textile factories. There was no time or energy left for the acquirement of an education. A very small portion of those interviewed attended the Russian elementary or high school. None had graduated from a Czarist school of higher learning, and not one came to this country as a trained professional.

The kheyder, the yeshive, the Russian elementary school, and the technical school were the best of which the poorer elements of the Jewish population in the old country could avail themselves.

Our study of the Hebrew educational background of the older generation of the family circle reveals the following:

80% attended kheyder
15% attended yeshive
5% attended Hebrew school.

Among them were those who likewise had a secular education, but their proportion is not large. Of these:

20% attended Russian elementary school,
1% attended technical school.

The above figures give an idea of the educational background of the male members of the family circle. The educational standing of the female members of the older generation was even lower. At a tender age they were harnessed to housework or factory labor. Giving girls an education was not considered a vital problem among Jewish parents. They were more concerned with educating their boys. The results among the women are, therefore, more negative, as shown by the following figures:

70% apparently had no Jewish education whatever,
20% attended the Jewish kheyder,
10% had private religious tutorship.

Only 10 percent of the women had attended Russian elementary school. The rest had no secular schooling whatever in their youth.

This does not mean that the older generation was not affected by outside cultural influences of a social-political character. Both the revolutionary movement against the Czar and Zionism influenced a number and stimulated them to become more familiar with the theoretical side of the respective movements. The influence of the [Jewish Labor] Bund was predominant. It is interesting to note that those who were under the influence of some social movement (in this case especially the Bund) were more literate, more cultured. In the privacy of their homes they would read literature tabooed by the authorities, and in public reading rooms and study circles they would peruse the better Yiddish literary works.

According to our study, at least fourteen percent of the older generation was under such a social-political influence. This is not disproportionate when it is remembered what a great risk an individual took in associating himself with the revolutionary movement.

Want, poverty, anti-Semitism, pogroms—these were circumstances that accounted for the lack of education and cultural upbringing on the part of the older generation of men and women belonging to our family circle—circumstances that inevitably have left their effects. The effects were profound, and, in the process of migrating and settling in a new land, they became more manifest.

> I landed in Boston. Immediately I went to New York to spend a day with my sister who was living on the lower East Side. The following day I was a boarder at the home of my brother in Brownsville. On the third day of my arrival in this country I was busy on a construction job laying bricks. I hardly had a chance to catch my breath . . .

Such is the account of one of the members of the family circle. At present he is in his fifties and considers himself well off financially. His English is imperfect and ungrammatical and his accent foreign. His Yiddish is a jargon of English and Yiddish words. He was amazed to hear the writer who was interviewing him speak flawless Yiddish. "Look! What a fine Yiddish he speaks," he said to his wife, "just as it is spoken in the old country."

Neither he nor his wife ever attended evening school in this country. He worked from ten to twelve hours a day. The more hours, the better. Money had to be saved in order to finance the passage of a kinsman from the old country. And those near and dear remaining abroad had to be helped occasionally. In those days the wages were small, the hours long, and when evening arrived he was too exhausted. His wife, too, was worn out after a day of cooking, scrubbing, and caring for the children.

These and similar arguments were heard every time we tried to explore the cultural status of the family. Not all versions were the same. But to the interviewer it was clear that the chief reasons for the lack of education were economic. Even in cases where there was more leisure and opportunities for cultural development, the urge for knowledge was neglected and dormant. In fact, some were not even conscious of their shortcomings.

There were, naturally, those among the members of the family circle who were avid for knowledge, who attended evening schools, learned English, read books, and in general prepared for a cultural life. But these we found in small number. Nevertheless, the rank and file of the members of our family circle are not entirely unlettered. Those who read a daily newpaper, listen to the radio, and patronize the movies and theaters do not necessarily lead a life devoid of culture.

One might ask, what do people seek for recreation? Do they select serious or light entertainment, aesthetic pleasure, or simply a good time? It appears that a great majority prefer the latter in the form of cheap Yiddish theater, average movies, light radio programs. Books are seldom read. The older generation is not vitally interested in Jewish or general cultural problems. Even among those families with libraries in their homes, the volumes contained in the bookcases are mostly textbooks, primers for children, English literature studied by school children, and books that are seldom touched but serve as decoration and fill empty spaces on the shelves.

A woman of the older generation, who reads a Yiddish paper daily, patronizes the Yiddish theater, and listens to Yiddish radio programs, gave the interviewer an account of a pogrom in Bialystok in a jargon that was a mixture of Russian, English, and Yiddish. Not one of the three languages has she been able to master, and she isn't even aware of the fact that she doesn't command one language that she can call her own.

Nevertheless, there are persons in the family circle who do manifest an interest in Jewish and general cultural questions, but they are exceptions.

The following table gives an idea of the schooling acquired by the older generation in this country:

Men
40% attended evening school classes in English,
6% attend WPA classes,
5% attended evening high school.

Women
15% attended evening courses,
12% attend WPA classes.

Not one of the women of the older generation got as far as evening high school. Twenty percent of the men and 25 percent of the women speak English fluently.

Our reports on books in the homes of the older generation reveal the following:
30% have books in English and Yiddish,
15% have books only in English,
12% have books mostly in Yiddish,
2% have religious books only.

The remaining 41 percent of the families have no library whatever.

The following shows the type of reading engaged in by the men of the older generation:
16% read books in both English and Yiddish.
4% read books only in Yiddish.
30% seldom read books.

25% do not read books at all.

25% not determined.

Not always was it possible to determine whether or not books were read; not always was it possible to find out what type of reading was indulged in. As far as we could determine, only sixteen percent of the families read modern fiction and classics, in both English and Yiddish. The remainder, it seems, read whatever falls into their hands, literature that is most likely of doubtful quality.

So much for the men. As for the women of the older generation, it was likewise difficult to come to any conclusions as to their type of reading. Of them:

14% read books in English.

 8% read books only in Yiddish.

18% read in both languages.

23% don't read any books.

37% not determined.

Most of the women who read books select the cheap novel as their reading fare. Only about six percent, according to our reports, read with a purpose the better, more serious books.

Most of the members of the older generation attend the Yiddish theaters:

35% patronize the better Yiddish theaters.

65% patronize the cheaper Yiddish theaters.

Of these, twenty percent also patronize English theaters, and ten percent like musical comedies in English.

Movies are attended by 90 percent of the older generation. Of these:

 8% prefer Yiddish films.

30% prefer the better English films.

12% have seen, and like to see, Soviet films.

The rest go to see any films that strike their fancy.

As to radios and the appreciation of music, the following table was compiled:

100% have radios in their homes,

16% like to listen to English programs only,

50% prefer light entertainment,

34% relish programs of classical music,

40% enjoy Yiddish programs.

 6% attend concerts of classical music,

10% go to the opera.

Newspaper reading, which is bound to influence the cultural life of the Jewish family of the older generation, is divided as follows:

Yiddish Newspapers

40% read the *Forward*,

35% read the *Day*,

12% read the *Jewish Morning Journal*,

 3% read the *Morning Freiheit*.

The English Press
20% read the *New York Times,*
15% read the *New York Post,*
10% read the *Daily News,*
6% read the *World-Telegram.*

English magazines are often found in the homes of the families, but a Yiddish magazine seldom. Most of the magazines read by children are of the pulp variety.

As to language used in the homes, the following has been compiled:

in 35% of the homes only Yiddish is spoken,
in 40% both Yiddish and English are spoken,
in 25% English only is spoken.

It is not unlikely that many members of the older generation have at various times striven to better their lot. The only indication we have of this is the attitude many of the older generation have assumed in regard to the education of their offspring. They want to make of their children what they themselves failed to achieve in their own youth. They sacrificed material comfort for the sake of their children's education, so that the latter might have a better chance in life. Needless to say, in America they have been able to accomplish far more for their children than their parents were able to do for them in the old country.

The Younger Generation

The young American generation of the family circle speaks little and has less to say. Its childhood experiences are not quite comparable with those of the older generation. They were not faced with the same economic handicaps and the paucity of opportunities for cultural development that thwarted their forebears in their youth. Cultural objectives that their parents never even dreamed of achieving in their youth came easily to the young Americans. Doors that were closed to the poor, especially the Jewish poor, in the European countries were here open to their offspring. When we say "open" we do not overlook the state of poverty which in most cases prevented parents from enabling their children to acquire a higher education along academic lines. Nor do we overlook those exclusive halls of learning which are open only to Jews who have the necessary funds and the social contacts to warrant their admission. Nevertheless, those parents who were strongly desirous of obtaining the proper education for their children, and those children who refused to be deterred in their efforts to acquire the knowledge they sought, managed somehow to find ample educational opportunities.

For the immigrant Jewish family the problem of giving its children an American secular education has not been quite as difficult as that of giving them a Jewish secular or a Jewish religious education. When one mentions this problem to the older generation, the reply is a shrug of the shoulders. "What can you expect," they say, "this is America." "Yes," they claim, "we tried." They sent their children to Hebrew school and to Talmud Torah—but nothing came of it.

Interest in the Yiddish language, Yiddish culture, and in problems of a purely Jewish nature has not been fostered and stimulated. Parents who, in most cases, were themselves unacquainted with Jewish culture, could hardly be expected to impart such knowledge to their children.

The young people know how to read and write a little Yiddish, but they seldom read it, much less write it. With their parents they converse in a jargon of mingled Yiddish and English. Outside their homes they cease to speak Yiddish and are prone to forget it entirely.

We found no serious friction between the older and youger generation regarding the use of Yiddish as a language. The children are tolerant of the language of their parents, but it cannot be denied that they regard Yiddish with indifference. This is primarily because the Yiddish that they hear in their homes is so mutilated that it must sound like gibberish. As a rule, the members of the younger generation have not learned to appreciate Yiddish as a pure, literary language.

But there are exceptions. There is the case of a young man in the family circle, native-born, who graduated from high school, who is well versed in English and in American literature, and who, in addition, maintains a profound interest in modern Yiddish literature. In his bookcase are volumes by Rosenfeld, Edelshtat, Nadir, Asch, Yossel Kotler and others. He derives the greatest pleasure from Kotler. He claims that he doesn't read assiduously as he is too busily occupied to become a scholar, but he finds time somehow to read all the essential Yiddish books and absorb their text. He speaks a pure and fluent Yiddish, is fond of the Yiddish theater, and attends Yiddish lectures.

How did he discover Yiddish and what aroused his interest, you may ask? Not directly through the interest and influence of his parents. They sent him to Talmud Torah where he learned to read and write Yiddish. Otherwise his interest in the language of his race would undoubtedly have languished, as in the case of most of the other members of the younger generation.

But one day he chanced to browse in a Jewish book shop to kill a little idle time. There, quite by accident, the true wealth and quality of Yiddish literature was unfolded before him. He picked up a book of Rosenfeld's poems and was astounded when the realization struck home that Yiddish in its highest form was a language of beauty and far from gibberish. Rosenfeld's poems inspired in him a true appreciation of the quality and genius of Yiddish literature. He is grateful, he says, to this chance perusal of a book which gave him a lasting interest in Yiddish, and hopes more young people will be similarly fortunate.

When there is a discord between the older and the younger generation, it is generally brought about because the parents resent their children's adoption of viewpoints that they consider impious and off the beaten path. We know of cases in which parents became incensed because their children brought radical literature into the home. This sometimes resulted in estrangement between parent and child. We also know of friction resulting from children's reading books that had no connection with their school courses. But the younger generation is not altogether to blame.

The following table shows the extent of Jewish education among the younger generation:

     30% attended kheyder.
     30% know how to read and write Yiddish slightly.
     10% attended a Hebrew school.
     4% attended a Workmen's Circle school.
     18% had no Jewish education at all.
     8% undetermined.

Although the cultural level among the Jewish youth is not a high one, and not even average, the majority of them received the education of an average American child. All graduated from public school. Of those who continued with their studies:

     60% attended high school.
     20% enrolled in colleges and universities.
     10% went to business schools.
     4% attended technical schools.

Many of them learned trades in order to fit themselves for employment as rapidly as possible, so that they could become economically independent. Many of those who attended college took their courses in the evening. In the daytime they found employment in offices and factories. During the summer months they often worked in resorts.

Not all of the younger generation manifested a desire for a strictly academic education and the acquirement of a professional status. Despite persuasion on the part of their parents to continue with their studies, they preferred to look for work. Their argument of late has often been,

> what's the use of studying to become a doctor, a lawyer, or a teacher when in a depression the ordinary factory worker has a better chance of earning a livelihood than a professionally trained person?

That this argument is not without logical basis cannot be denied when it is observed that quite a number of those who attended universities and obtained an academic degree eventually were forced to learn a trade when despair led them to abandon hope of ever finding employment in their chosen profession.

Of those who graduated from colleges, one-third could find no opportunity to practice their chosen professions and were obliged to accept employment in offices and stores.

Perhaps it is not more than mere coincidence that the reports do not show even one case of creative artistic effort on the part of the younger generation. There are no painters, actors, poets, musicians or dancers. One girl did aspire to become a danseuse, but after a short-lived effort took a job in a factory.

What type newspaper does the young generation read? Superficially it would appear that tabloids constitute the sole reading fare, but the reports show that:

30% read the *Daily News.*
20% read the *New York Post.*
18% read the *New York Times.*
15% read the *Daily Mirror.*
8% read the *World-Telegram.*
2% read the *Daily Worker.*

In recreation the movies take top rank. Almost everyone of the younger generation is a movie fan. Although movies can be, and sometimes are, a constructive part of the cultural-recreational life of an individual, the younger generation eschews the more serious drama and classic entertainment, such as interpretive and aesthetic dancing.

Their preferences are distributed as follows:

20% like musical comedies.
20% like the more serious English dramas.
3% patronize the Yiddish stage.
30% prefer light musicals.
45% enjoy programs of classical music.

Such is the educational and cultural status of the younger generation of the family circle. From the reports it can be seen that the native-born Jewish youth has not become conscious of its kinship to its people, a people with its own language, its own culture, and its own life problems, which merit more consideration and more serious esteem from the young people.

8. Three Generations

The First Generation: Neshke

Two things impress the visitor upon entering Neshke's apartment on Dumont Avenue in the Brownsville section of Brooklyn. The first is the super-abundance of framed photographs: bridal groups, couples, children and individuals. Many of these line the walls of the four-room apartment; others are arranged on the buffet, dresser, dining table, and whatever other flat-topped piece of furniture there is in the house. Over two thousand additional photos are stored in trunks. A large photograph, three by three feet, in color, of Neshke and her late husband, hangs over the sofa in the combination dining and sitting room.

The prevalence of so many photographs can be explained by the fact that Neshke has eight married sons, twenty-two grandchildren, and two great-grandchildren.

The second impressive thing in Neshke's apartment is the large assortment of red and pink crepe flowers and flowery decorations adorning each of the rooms. The kitchen, which one enters first, is festooned with flowers. Bouquets of imitation carnations and roses fill the vases on the two kitchen tables; the linoleum has scarlet flowery designs and the oilcloth decorating the closet shelves has almost similar patterns; the cups and saucers have scarlet borders, as do the glasses; the criss-cross curtains are tucked in with scarlet sashes on whose edges scarlet crepe carnations have been pinned.

In the combination dining and sitting room the carpet is crimson, dotted with flowers and gay decorations. The parlor suite is upholstered in red mohair on which rest a collection of red pillows studded with bright-colored flowery designs. On the dining table stands a large vase filled with imitation flowers.

In the main bedroom, the twin beds have white bedspreads sprinkled with an assortment of floral decorations. A boudoir doll, with flowery headdress, reclines on each bed.

Even the bathroom, leading off the kitchen, has a quota of flowery decorations on the window and shower curtains, bath mat, and oilcloth lining the shelves of the medicine chest. As a final touch, the shower curtain is tucked on one side with a fitting scarlet sash and crepe carnation.

From her early childhood Neshke had an innate love for flowers and bright colors. As a little girl she used to gather flowers in the field to decorate her home. In winter when there weren't any flowers to be picked she would make imitation flowers out of crepe. Perhaps it was an escape from the drab surroundings of poverty that prompted her into a world of flowers. Or perhaps it was her artistic temperament that had its expression in this form. Who knows but that, under less grinding poverty, she might have been a painter of flowers and landscapes?[1]

At twelve, Neshke was sent to work in a cotton factory in order to supplement her father's meager earnings. He was a coachman, barely making enough to support his wife and children. Never once was she inside a schoolroom. Her teen years were spent in a dusty factory, sorting cotton remnants. There was no time for play. In the evening, after work, she would help her mother in her household chores.

In the long hours of monotonous factory work, Neshke would dream of flowers and sunshine. Not until she was twenty did romance come into her life. Her "fairy prince" was a young Bialystok coachman whom she met at her uncle's house. It was a case of love at first sight, and before many weeks had passed, Neshke heard the magic words, "Will you be my wife?" She replied in the affirmative even though she knew he was due for three years military service. Luckily, he drew the number that exempted him from army service, and the marriage was celebrated with great rejoicing.[2]

Children came to Neshke one after the other. She had thirteen, all but one being boys, of whom eight are living today. The more children that came the more mouths there were to feed, and the irregular earnings of Neshke's husband were insufficient to support so large a family. And so the devoted wife and mother was obliged to return to her job in the cotton factory, to bolster her husband's income. The older children were trained to take care of the younger ones while the mother was out at work. Upon returning from work Neshke would do the family cooking for the following day.[3]

On Thursday nights she would work particularly hard, preparing for the Sabbath. She would bake her khales [braided Sabbath loaves], roast the goose, cook fish, make noodles, and prepare the compote. The next day, Friday, she would be back at the job in the cotton factory. Not even pregnancy interrupted her outside employment. She almost had her youngest baby while at work at the factory.

On Saturday night, after the havdole [the ceremony performed at the close of the Sabbath], Neshke would resume the hobby she had maintained since childhood, that of making imitation flowers, paper doilies, and doodads of all kinds. Before holidays she would make pretty paper baskets which she would hang all over the crowded three-room apartment. She would decorate the walls with cardboard shelvings on which she would place a conglomeration of paper dolls and toys created by her.

In the spring of 1906 Neshke's first-born, Morris, left for America. That summer witnessed the pogrom in Bialystok. It was Thursday and Neshke was at work as usual, in the cotton factory situated on the outskirts of Bialystok. Suddenly an alarming bit of news raced through the factory. The pogrom was on. Everybody dashed for a hiding place. Neshke, together with two other women workers, hid in the enormous factory stove that heated the plant during the winter months. For two whole days the pogrom raged and for two whole days Neshke and her companions remained sequestered in the stove. A sympathetic Pole brought them food, but Neshke's mind was not on food but on the fate of her family. "Were they molested by the pogromchikes? Are they still alive? Oh, God, have mercy on them!"

Not until late Saturday afternoon was the frantic mother able to emerge from her unusual hiding place. On the way home she forgot about the frightful experience she had gone through these past forty-eight hours. She couldn't run fast enough to her home.[4]

To her great joy she found everybody home and well. Her apartment had been overlooked by the marauders. After eating and resting, the happy mother was told the story of the pogrom as seen and heard from inside the barricaded apartment. When the pogrom first started only two of the boys, eleven-year-old Nathan and thirteen-year-old Artshik, were home. They were soon joined by Louis and Velvl, dragging their four-year-old brother Izzy with them. The father was the last to come home. He barricaded the gate in front of the house with the aid of his wagon. The horse was deposited in the stable.

Soon shots were heard ringing out in all directions, followed by piercing screams from the victims. The children hid behind the stove which was to serve as a buffer against bullets. The father himself refused to seek shelter; he paced back and forth nervously, worrying over the fate of his wife.

The commotion outside continued unabated all through the night, all of the following day, and reached its climax that night. The boys fell asleep from sheer exhaustion on the floor behind the stove. Suddenly a deafening shot rang outside the house. Little Artshik woke up screaming and ran to his father crying, "I'm scared, I'm scared!"

From that night on Artshik was never the same. At night he would suffer from nightmares. As time progressed he got worse and died at fifteen in a fit of epilepsy which was ascribed to the scare he experienced the Friday night of the pogrom.

This was the first hard blow in Neshke's life. But Artshik was not the only victim of the pogrom. There was another victim in the form of an unborn child. Neshke was in the fifth month of pregnancy when the pogrom broke out. The excitement and discomfort of hiding in the stove caused her to have a miscarriage a few days later.

Before the pogrom year was over, Sam, her other son, was sent to America to join Morris. Neshke's life resumed its daily routine, of working in the cotton factory and preparing her next day's meals just before she went to bed. She did her shopping on the way home. Nathan and Izzy would clean the frozen fish she would bring home. The two boys were also very helpful in scrubbing floors and tidying up the three-room apartment for which the rent was sixty rubles a year. When their mother was too tired to cook their next day's meal, they volunteered to cook it themselves. A good part of the day the children spent at kheyder, and so they weren't quite alone all day.

The peaceful existence of the family was interrupted by the Great War which brought misery and despair in its wake to millions of homes in Europe. Velvl, being of military age, was the first to be recruited. For three months he wrote regularly twice a week and then stopped abruptly.

Weeks passed into months and still there was no word from him. The mother's wet pillows spoke only too plainly of the sleepless nights she spent in weeping and worrying about her son.

"Where are you, my darling? Are you well? May the evil spirit pass over you without touching you!" was the worried mother's fervent prayer.

And when she finally fell asleep the vision of Velvl appeared before her. He was home, helping her to spread out the dough for the matzos, shoving the matzos into the stove; or he would be helping her with the doodads that she had just made, hanging them on the walls or suspending them from the ceiling.

The morrow would bring fresh hopes. Surely, there must be a letter from Velvl this morning. The mail comes and brings letters from Morris and Sam in America, but none from Velvl. She puts on her shawl and runs to the post office. Maybe the postman failed to deliver her boy's letter. "Revered sir," she approaches the postmaster, "are you positive there is no letter?" The postmaster goes over the mail and returns with a negative answer, apparently annoyed at the woman's persistence. The sorrowing mother bows her head and walks out of his office. "Tomorrow, surely tomorrow, I will hear from him," she consoles herself.

Tomorrow came and another tomorrow and many more tomorrows and still there was no word from Velvl. "Oh Heavenly Father, have mercy on me," was the distracted mother's prayer. "Let us have one word, just one word from my son—even a bad word!"

And the morrows rolled into years—one, two, three, four and five. Neshke no longer prayed for Velvl's well-being. She was positive he was dead and lighted a memorial lamp in his honor. The equally brokenhearted father was saying kadish in his memory.

Neshke forgot to laugh; she even forgot the hunger that was gnawing at her vitals, for those were days of famine.

Then one day—it was Friday evening—Neshke was lighting candles. During her ceremonial prayer she broke out in uncontrollable weeping and praying for her son's soul. Suddenly there was a loud knock at the door. She wiped her eyes and opened the door.

"Velvl!" she shrieked and fell into a dead faint.[5]

Velvl had finally returned. He had been kept a prisoner in a German concentration camp all these years.

Velvl's parents were not the only ones who waited, hoped, and lost hope. There was a girl, a sixteen-year-old orphan, in whom he was interested and whom he intended to make his bride some day. Shortly before he went off to war he brought her to his home and introduced her to his family. Neshke took a great liking to this girl, and every morning on her way to work she would stop at the dressmaking establishment in which the girl was employed and bring her her lunch. As time wore on the two would share each other's anxiety over Velvl's well-being.

After four years had passed without word from Velvl it was taken for granted that he was lost forever. By this time Nathan had grown to manhood, and he began to take an interest in Velvl's girl friend. The two began to go out and, after some months had passed, found that they were in love with each other. Neshke was only too happy to have this girl for her daughter-in-law, and the marriage, though a quiet one, was consummated with great satisfaction to everyone in the household.

And so, he who came back from the dead was greeted with hysterical joy mixed with considerable embarrassment—Velvl's girl married to his younger brother!

Velvl could not stay at home. It was too much for him. He left for America and settled in Montreal where he is living to this day. He is married to a Montreal girl and is the father of five children.

Neshke's anxieties were by no means over. For more than three years she had not heard from her son Louis, who joined his brothers Morris and Sam in New York just before the war broke out. The last she heard was that Louis was very ill. During the war when transatlantic mail was interrupted, she was unable to get further word as to his illness. In due time she was convinced that he too was no longer living. And the stricken father said kadish after him too. Finally, when mail service with America was resumed, the good word from Louis came, that he was alive and well and cured of his ailment. To reassure them, he sent along his photo taken with his brothers.

In 1921 Sam and Morris, who already had a prospering clothing business of their own, sent for their parents and their younger brothers, Sydney and Henry, who were minors, and the quartet set sail for a new life in a new world.

It was a life of peace and prosperity, of rest and recreation that awaited Neshke, a life she had hardly known before. Her husband, after years of driving a horse and wagon in rain, snow, sleet, and frost now could live in quiet retirement. He could spend all his time in the besmedresh [prayer and study house] and study the holy books, an ambition he had cherished all his life. Back home he was a bal-tfile [prayer leader] in the Bialystok synagogue, but now his voice was too weak for this type of service. It was this synagogue, composed largely of members of his family and that of his wife, that served as the nucleus of the present family circle.[6]

For fifteen years Neshke was to live the happiest years of her life, years during which there were marriages, brisn [circumcisions], pidyen habens [traditional ceremonies for first-born sons], confirmation parties, and holiday festivals. On Passover all the sons and their wives and their children would assemble at the home of their parents for the seyder. Neshke would patter around in all her glory, anticipating the great event. She would prepare the choicest of dishes for her dear ones, her daughters-in-law lending a helping hand. During one of these seyders, movies were taken of the ritual feast, showing Neshke's husband in his ceremonial vestments.

As the years rolled by Neshke and her husband had more and more nakhes [proud enjoyment] from their children, particularly from their sons Morris and Sam, whose business grew and prospered. Both Morris and Sam were noble in their treatment of their parents. Each week their bookkeeper, upon drawing up the weekly pay roll, would make out checks for their parents, a check for twenty dollars for the mother's upkeep and an extra check for the father, so that he could enjoy the synagogue and contribute to the various welfare funds raised by the congregation.

Four years ago a heavy cloud came over Neshke. It was the death of her husband who passed away at 74. To this day she has not recovered from the shock. "I lost a gem, a precious gem," she despairs as tears fill her eyes. "Life has never been the same since . . ."

But she is not altogether alone in her old age. Her widowed sister, Bessie, two years her senior, has joined her, and the two live contentedly together, sharing in the cooking, cleaning, and household expense. The twenty dollar check, sent jointly by Morris and Sam, continues to arrive punctually every week, and Neshke is spared the pangs of economic insecurity in her old age.[7]

Her apartment is situated diagonally across the street from that of her son, Nathan, and her other son, Isidor, lives but one block away. Her proximity to her two sons makes it easy for them and their families to visit her several times a day. On Sundays she is taken for long drives in Nathan's or Isidor's car, and once a week she visits Morris who embraces her with all the warmth of a doting son. "Cheer up, mother," he says, "stop worrying, we'll always take good care of you."

Neshke maintains very friendly relations with each of her daughters-in-law. On Fridays she sends them samplings of her famous kugel and Sabbath cakes. They in turn send her their favorite delicacies which they know will please the palate of their mother-in-law.

Despite her age, Neshke has a fair and youthful complexion. One could hardly believe that this kindly face had been through so much hardship and terror. Her gray hair, combed into a knot on top of her head, adds a touch of aged beauty to this matriarch. Being short and rather stout, she is the typical Jewish grandmother.

To this day Neshke's love for flowers and bright colors has not abated. She spends her spare time in making imitation flowers, if not for herself, for her many descendants.

At age seventy-four she enjoys fair health. At times she suffers from the effects of high blood pressure and a peculiar buzzing in her ears. But she rarely misses a meeting of the family circle she belongs to and takes a keen interest in the affairs of the organization.

Neshke has never learned to speak English or to read or write any language. Thanks to the Yiddish programs on the radio, she is able to keep abreast of world events. The tragic fate of Jews in Central Europe saddens her and at the same time reminds her how fortunate she is to be living in this country. She has much to be thankful for, thankful that her eight sons have "made good" in the New World. They are model sons and husbands, and she is proud of them.

And so this brave matriarch, surrounded as she is by her doting near and dear ones, is facing the sunset of her life amid peace and security—a far cry from the days of poverty and terror in Bialystok.

The Second Generation: Isidor

Isidor came into this world sixty-three years ago, and was named Itsikl. In the poor Jewish quarter of Bialystok there was an abundance of such offspring. Jewish economic life was meager and unsettled; nobody ever bothered to bring order into it. Jews begot children indiscriminately. In the course of time narrow, winding market streets were filled with children, stepmothers, and wailing chants.

At home Itsikl was one of eight children. The father, a Hebrew teacher, was forever ailing; the mother, bent under a sack stuffed full of vegetables, would go knocking at the doors of the rich, offering her wares for sale. The yoke of life was heavy upon her.

Children of a house which consists of a single room mature quickly, and each one plans in secret to build up a world of his own.

Itsikl attended kheyder until the age of ten. Afterwards he learned the trade of masonry. He was a strong lad and aspired to achieve something in life. He grew in will power and stubbornness. He was a man who some day would make something of himself.[8]

The father was ailing. The mother trudged from village to town, bent under the weight of her burdensome sack, and would often be gone for days. But a child does need someone's care . . . so Itsikl happened to meet a cousin.

Itsikl was ten, and his cousin, Ester-Khaytshe, nine. They met at a birthday party in Zabludow, not far from Bialystok. At the first glance their heartbeats quickened and they were filled with wonder and mystery.

The two children met from time to time and talked. The boy revealed to her his plans:

He would live in a house of two rooms, not one, like his father. He would be no Hebrew-teaching drudge, but a carpenter like her father. He would be the one to provide for his family. Ester-Khaytshe listened, and looked up to him. Under her gaze, Itsikl felt himself growing up, like a man with responsibilities.

His older brother, Jacob Aaron, was studying at the yeshive. His second brother took up tailoring and a third, shoemaking. A half-sister had left for

Palestine and she wrote that things were not going well with her, but she would by no means return home even if they sent her a steamship ticket.

Standing on the scaffold, Itsikl was laying the bricks while his thoughts wandered. With each growing house his plans grew. His grandfather and great-grandfather had lived in the neighborhood for a hundred years. They were among the first settlers there. Itsikl wanted to continue the line. He would build himself a house facing that of his future father-in-law, on the soil where every pebble and grain of sand were familiar to him and in plain sight of the townspeople . . .

But it was going from bad to worse for the Jews. A Jewish lad who worked all day long and far into the evenings, or one who returned home late at night from a private lesson, would frequently be chased by drunken policemen with unsheathed sabers, calling out "Zhidi! Zhidi!" (Sheenies! Sheenies!) Itsikl, like other Jewish boys, was afraid of drunkards, dogs, and the pitch-black nights which shrouded the unlighted, twisted Jewish alleys . . .

He talked about these things with Ester-Khaytshe. He pictured for her a world without drunkards and dogs. Strolling with her along the narrow paths in the woods, he pointed to the sky where it fused with the earth. He would gladly take her there if only he could. Truly, he meant every word he said . . .

Ester-Khaytshe had a stepmother, and was one of eight children in the house. It was "mine and yours" not "ours." Her own mother died in childbirth (a common occurrence in that town). At an early age she became a seamstress. A radiant girl, not fully grown, with dark tresses and arched eyebrows, she sat in the workshop together with other girls and sang songs about orphans . . .

Years passed. Itsikl had become a craftsman, earning good wages, and Ester-Khaytshe learned how to sew with ease. They considered themselves betrothed, and the rest of the townspeople looked approvingly upon the match. Only the marriage brokers were trying to spoil it. They could not understand why such a desirable engagement should have been arranged without their intercession, and with no profit to them. They tried to interest Itsikl in girls of wealthy families, especially now that he had reached the age of compulsory military service. They were ready to help him dodge it by attaching him to another family as an only son. But Itsikl would have none of their meddling.

At twenty-one, Itsikl was a medium-sized, broad-boned young man with a sharply pointed chin and a wise look in his eyes. Ester-Khaytshe, somewhat smaller in stature, had grown more womanly. They talked about his imminent service in the army, and decided that he would not maim himself, as others did, in order to be rejected. If it was God's will to go through with it, he would do so; and, with God's help, he would return and marry her.

Itsikl was conscripted into the army for four years.

While in service he learned to read musical notes and became a member of the military band. At the end of his term he was honorably discharged, came home and married his bride. The wedding ceremony was performed in the Jewish traditional manner. Within the year a child was born to them.

It was all right for a man to serve in the army four years, Itsikl reflected, and they were difficult years. Yet on the day after his discharge, he was not permitted to stay in Moscow even one extra hour. The Czar suddenly remembered that he was a Jew. How could anyone be patriotically inclined to such a country?

This led the young couple to the thought of emigrating to America. True, they had a nicely furnished home and an infant. But there was no future for them.

By that time Itsikl had a brother and a sister living in New York. His brother-in-law wrote him that he was a hatter, and that in America one finds no gold lying about in the streets, but if one is ready to work hard one can earn a livelihood.

In 1904, at the age of 26, Itsikl left for New York, traveling at his own expense. He disembarked at Ellis Island with only five rubles to his name. He sent a wire to his brother-in-law announcing his arrival but was released from Ellis Island before the telegram was delivered.

The moment he was set free he was overcome by a sudden longing for his wife. Tears welled up in his eyes; but he was not going to weep. He picked up his braided suitcase and boarded the ferry to Battery Park. There he was directed to the Second Avenue elevated train which brought him to the First Street station.

At the given address on Second Street, Itsikl mounted five flights of stairs, when he discovered that his sister lived on the second floor.

He knocked and, like a beggar, stood in the doorway. But his sister, brother-in-law, and nephews gave him a rousing reception. For a week afterwards they plied him with questions about everybody and everything back home, and they shed tears . . . During that time he felt very sleepy. The family explained that all "greenhorns" feel that way the first few days in this country. "One has to get used to the American air."

When the first week was over, Itsikl put on old clothes, and started working on a scaffold. A friend from his home town took him to Brownsville. There, he got a job and found a lodging place.

In those days, workers in the building trade earned $5.60 a day, for it was one of the better-paid trades. There was plenty of work to be had, for Brownsville was in the midst of a real-estate boom. But in order to obtain a job, one was required to declare his intention of becoming a citizen of the United States and join a union. Thus Itsikl did, and he changed his name to Isidor.

Isidor became a boarder. He worked all day, and wrote letters to his Ester-Khaytshe at night.

". . . It won't be long now," he reassured her. With the first few dollars he saved up, he would send for her. Let her pay no attention to the talk of neighbors. He would keep his word as ever . . .

After fifteen months he sent for his wife and 28-month-old son. Isidor installed them on Pitkin Avenue in a four-story tenement, paying twelve dollars a month for four rooms.

The streets in that part of Brooklyn were not yet paved. The houses were without electric light or steam heat. The only bit of civilization illuminating the place was gas light.

Isidor had worked uninterruptedly for twelve years. During that time four more children were born into the family, augmenting the needs for food and clothing. With the outbreak of the War in 1914, Isidor lost his job. He made up his mind to go to Perryville, Maryland. There he found employment, for the government was building an ammunition plant.

"How did you find out about Perryville?"

"Well, there was talk among the workers that jobs go begging there. My wife and children wanted food. . . .

"A Jew," continued Isidor, "does not like roaming about. But if he learns of a place where he can earn his bread, he immediately sets out in that direction."

In 1918 he returned to New York where he was joined by his three brothers, who emigrated from Bialystok. One day they decided that it was high time to give up toiling for others, and to establish some kind of business of their own. That same year they became partners in a garage business.

Isidor spent eight years in the garage business without attaining the desired proficiency.

In 1927 he became an entrepreneur, a builder of houses. He reached his goal at last. He materialized his boyhood dreams. "I built up a great many houses in Brooklyn," he related.

> I can't say that I didn't make money. I made plenty. For years I was busy, head over heels. As you see me, I, Itsikl of Bialystok, helped to build up the greatest city in the world!
>
> At one time my savings amounted to from $25,000 to $30,000. This I invested in empty lots. The crash in 1929 cleaned me out of every cent I saved up. It forced me back to my discarded tools.
>
> Now, after working again for years, and with the children bringing home their "pay," we managed to save up $3,000, own an unpaid-for family house and a car.
>
> I have good children, and we are indebted to no one. We are in good standing in our societies. If it comes to giving charity, we are first on the donors' list. People on our block still regard us as wealthy. . . . Thank God we are not in Europe!

Isidor takes pride in America, although he can hardly be taken for what is commonly known as an American. At home he speaks with the children a conglomeration of English and Yiddish. He tried to give them a religious education, although he himself omits the synagogal service, except on the high holidays.

Speaking of Americanism, Isidor is at a loss to explain the term. He has lived in this country the greatest part of his life. He worked all the time, which means that he contributed something to the country. What if he doesn't speak English well? Did he have the time to learn? Now he is a man in years, and the mind is not so easily receptive. . . . Besides, he has very little time. He has helped build America, and he votes for what he considers the best candidates. Isn't that Americanism?

With regard to anti-Semitism, Isidor feels it is best not to think of it. Why deny that of late a number of virulent Jew baiters have emerged and they are barking up a tree? It is just as well that they have no teeth with which to bite.

Isidor's social interests are focused on the Bialystok landsmanshaft society, the union, and the family circle.[9] He is pleased with the honor of having been an official of the society for six years, and of having his name and those of his sons carved on the cemetery gate of the family circle. That is quite an honor. He and his favorite son are the founders of the family circle.

Isidor is satisfied with his life's work. He has led his family life according to plan, and in his heart he enjoys a rare serenity. He built his house in the spirit of his tradition and lineage, and he has provided himself and family with a burial plot in the family circle cemetery. A curious thing how immigrant Jews are inclined to magnify the idea of possessing their own burial ground, which amounts to almost a fetish. Probably because in life they have the feeling of being uprooted, and look forward to death when they will lie side by side in a place that will be eternally theirs.

Isidor's children and grandchildren will follow in his footsteps. Only they speak a different language—English. But intrinsically they are knit together by their kinship and their daily needs. They are a simple, industrious family.

Ester-Khaytshe bears her share in the family responsibilities. She did not go to work because she had to take care of the home and children.[10] Today she lives in an apartment of four rooms, her own house, on Rockaway Parkway, and is obviously more comfortable than when she was on Pitkin Avenue where she lived years ago, paying twelve dollars a month.

She is the prudent housewife who constantly straightens out things. Her world is made up of the children, keeping the apartment clean, cooking, and seeing that everything is in order. Each room and compartment shimmers with cleanliness, giving one the caressing feeling of genial hospitality. Ester-Khaytshe runs her home on twenty-five dollars a week, i.e., for herself, husband, and three children (two are married). She observes the dietary laws, and blesses the candles on Sabbath eve.

She has outside interests, too. She belongs to a ladies' auxiliary and attends its regular meetings. In the matter of the children she has been quicker of perception than her husband. "A mother will be a mother, regardless." Instinctively she has sensed the new trend in America. Yet, she is not very talkative. She has neither the words, nor the courage to speak up. She lets her husband do the talking. He is loquacious, a talent he apparently acquired at her expense. She has respected him for more than thirty years. In return he never regarded her as his "footstool." He has shared everything with her on the basis of equality. This may be seen from the way she reacts to things, the way she restrains him with a look when he is about to say too much.

Nathan, their oldest son, is now thirty-six. When he was a youngster his father was still a "greenhorn." He could not, or would not, understand the ways of an American boy who loves to play ball, and be an all-around athlete.

Nathan tells of an incident when his sister broke a vase. Father suspected him, for who else could be so reckless if not the "ball player?" That evening he was pulled out of bed and whipped by his furious father. Nathan can't forget it.

Like his father, Nathan is a stubborn man. But while his father overcame all obstacles, Nathan fell short of his goal. As a result, he is taciturn and a prey to his moods.

He is a milk route driver, working at night and sleeping during the day. It is hard work, but he is contented.

He is a member of the union as well as the family circle, but has no time to be active in either. He leads a worker's existence. He and his wife take a keen interest in their son who is reaching the age of bar-mitsve and who attends Hebrew school.

The family regards Isidor's second son, Jack, with admiration. At twenty-three he is a graduate pharmacist, well built and of medium height. He gives the impression of being a well-behaved, intelligent young man.

Jack started to work as a shipping clerk when he was sixteen. This he did out of a desire for independence, and not because of need.

He was born here, finished public school, high school, and Brooklyn College. While going to college, he worked on Saturdays. Vacation time he worked as a waiter at summer resorts in the Catskill Mountains. In his spare time he learned how to read and write Yiddish. Now he reads very little. "There's no time for it, working twelve hours a day."

He does not encounter anti-Semitism to any great extent. But in the store he often hears Gentile customers say, "Jack, you are all right, not at all like other Jews."

Jack does not fraternize with his fellow pharmacists. He has his more personal friends. He is active in no particular organization though he feels strongly as a Jew and as an American. He, too, is a member of the family circle, but seldom attends meetings. He prefers to go to the movies, to a dance, and sometimes takes in a Yiddish play.

In appearance Jack resembles his father except that his features are more delicate. He is much less inclined to athletics than his younger brother, Harold. It would seem that the family, by showing him singular deference, placed a kind of restraint on him. His every word is taken as a weighty pronouncement.

Harold is twenty-one, the youngest of the family, and of average height. There is immense strength in his face and shoulders, and sinew in his every movement.

At the age of twelve he worked as a shipping clerk and at present is employed in a ladies' underwear factory. He is the only man among one hundred women operators, and earns sixteen dollars a week. He brings his "pay" home for which his mother provides him with food, clothing, shelter, and also manages to put some money aside for him. He enjoys going to the movies and playing ball. At home he is called the "baby," but he doesn't mind.

He, too, had attended Hebrew school, but remembers nothing except that Hebrew is a language. He does not believe in joining unions, and has no desire to advance himself. His only ambition is to become a champion baseball player. He reads the tabloids, that is, the pictures more than the lines, and the comic strips rather than the stories.

Anna is the home type of girl. She sits in a corner, and is ill at ease in the presence of a stranger. Her boy friend is a furrier and, like herself, American born.

She is about five feet four inches in height, and slender. Her oval face has fine lines, and her dark hair is bobbed.

Anna works as a bookkeeper in the office of an export house. After office hours she comes home and helps her mother in the kitchen.[11] The menfolk dominate the family. Mother and daughter are accustomed to doing their work in silence.

Anna, like her older married sister, Shirley, and like her mother, intends to observe the dietary laws, and bless the candles. Judaism and Americanism are interrelated in her mind. She knows that foreigners like her father have helped to build America. She therefore looks upon them with a deep-seated respect. They came here and reconstructed their lives with their bare ten fingers.

At Isidor's home they speak highly of Shirley's husband who is a silk salesman. "A 'silken' young man, eh?" remarks Isidor.

Shirley is now thirty-three, her husband, thirty-five. Eleven years ago they met for the first time at a banquet given by the Knights of Pythias. They fell in love at first sight, and married two years later. Two children were born to them. One is seven years old, and the other, three. The task of bringing them up is beginning to tell on Shirley. Her shoulders are drooping. But she doesn't mind. She feels she was born for the burden. Her life revolves around her husband, the two children, and a few neighbors.

Shirley occupies an apartment of four rooms for which she pays forty-seven dollars a month. She has plenty to do, caring for the house, the children, and her husband. At times the work falls hard on her. But her husband, Morris, often comes to her assistance. After she serves him his dinner, he puts the children to bed while she washes the dishes.

Morris was born in Russia. He was only two years in this country when he met Shirley. Impelled by a longing for homelike surroundings, he was happy to be associated with a domestic family. He had no time for any other kind of social life. For a time he worked for others; later he operated his own business, and now he is in the silk line.

He earns on the average forty dollars a week. This takes care of household expenses, insurance policies, doctors' bills, and other items. "One can't save money on that kind of a salary." Shirley induced him to join the family circle. He is glad he did.

Morris speaks English rather well, drawing on a sizable vocabulary. He picked up the language in his business and at evening school. At home he sits without a jacket in an easy chair and likes to tell how as a boy he wrote jingles while transporting sacks of grain on the Russian railways, and how he worked in a laundry in Paris. Once in a while, he says, he drops in to see a Yiddish play, and looks into a Yiddish newspaper whenever he visits his father-in-law a few blocks away.

Isidor, the one time Itsikl of Bialystok, now father of a branched-out family, gives the impression of a man who is standing firmly on the ground. One can easily imagine him in work clothes, with hammer and chisel in hand. Wherever a man like him settles, he strives to build his own house and put a fence around his own cultivated garden.

A family like Isidor's is undistinguished. Its life seldom glows with a holiday spirit. On the surface such a family makes no sensational contributions to the world . . .

Isidor started to work when he was ten. He served four years in the army, fell in love at a very young age, and realized his dogged ambition. He built houses, owned a garage, sold it, made money, lost money, and now is at work again, and active in organizations—what more can a man do?

Isidor and his wife have bowed to the influence of the New World, America. Essentially they are characteristic of their generation.

The Third Generation: Nathan

Ever since he could remember, Nathan was afraid of policemen. As a little boy his mother used to scare him into obedience by threatening to call the corner policeman, and since that time all policemen were bogeymen in his imagination. Little did he dream that someday he himself would be a policeman, pounding his beat on the sidewalks of Brownsville, toying with his nightstick, and seeing that all was well.[12]

Being a policeman was a far cry from what Nathan set out to be—an architect. All his youth he dreamed of designing beautiful homes. They would be superior to the rows of tenements that lined the streets of Brownsville in which he was born and raised. They would be surrounded with gardens and sunshine. They would possess every form of convenience that would add to the comfort and joy of living. And someday he would design the home of his bride . . .[13]

Thus did Nathan dream. But he was not only a dreamer. He believed in carrying his dreams into reality. Nothing could interfere with his plans, not even his father's inability to finance him through college where he could study architecture. He decided to work his way through college. And this he did by working as a bricklayer in the daytime and studying at night. And so in the daytime he helped to build houses and in the evening he learned to design them. It was hard going, but worth it.

Came the year 1930 and Nathan graduated from Cooper Union with honors. He was a full-fledged architect now, and at last his dreams were realized. But, alas, depression had set in, and the field for new architects was practically a closed one. Even those who had been in the field for years suddenly found themselves left in the cold. New houses weren't being built at the time. The crisis was growing . . .

Nathan had to look for something else and forget about his architecture, his life-long dreams and aspirations. His father, a garage owner, had friends in the police department, who prevailed on the young man to try for the police examinations. After all, there was nothing like trying.

Nathan happened to be athletically inclined. As a child he liked to play games with other children. Baseball was his favorite pastime. He grew up to be a tall man, of exceptional physique. He had no difficulty in passing the physical part of the police examination. The written test he likewise passed with high marks.

Came the day when Nathan put on his police uniform. It was a memorable day. He still remembers how self-conscious he felt that day. He thought everybody was looking at him and laughing at his awkward appearance. But when he reminded himself that at last he had acquired a secure existence for the rest of his life, he was thankful that he had been accepted on the force. True, he wasn't going to design those beautiful homes he dreamed of all his life, but, instead, he was going to preserve the peace and safety of Brownsville.

Up to his thirteenth birthday, Nathan was religiously inclined. Religion stirred his imagination. He liked to watch his mother bless the candles on Friday evenings, and on holidays he would join his father at the synagogue services. It became a habit with him to observe the dietary laws and not to eat bareheaded.

After having gone through the ceremony of bar-mitzve, he gradually freed himself from the religious moods. He now began to read scientific books, also classic and contemporary literature. He became an avid reader. He ceased to take part in the synagogue services, and broke the dietary laws whenever he ate outside his home. This often brought him in conflict with his parents who weren't exactly orthodox, but feared the possible effect of his unorthodox conduct on his younger brother and sister. However, his mother had no desire to drive him from the house, and wisely refrained from making an open issue of it. She ignored his infractions, and let well enough alone.

His father frowned on his intellectual pursuits. One day, in a rage, he picked up a stack of his son's magazines and books, raced down to the cellar and tossed them into the burning furnace. That scene will always be vivid in

Nathan's memory. How he raced after his father and managed to save Walt Whitman's poems from the fire!

Nathan has been on the police force for nine years. Those were interesting years, which he would not have missed for anything, what with observing life in all its aspects—poverty, accidents, deaths, and delinquency and crime in all its forms. To him the police force has been a great school, one that has taught him to understand life as it is lived.

And while pounding his beat, Nathan made a discovery that has practically revolutionized his inner life, one that has opened new horizons to him.

His beat in Brownsville was in a neighborhood where, as a youngster, he used to go to Hebrew School and learned to read Yiddish, a language he neglected soon after becoming bar-mitzve. There he chanced on a Yiddish book shop whose window attracted him because it gave him an opportunity to read the titles of the books exhibited and thereby put his knowledge of reading Yiddish into practice. He was amazed how much he still remembered.

One day he decided to step into the bookshop and glance through the books. In the narrow, dimly lighted shop he experienced a sense of surprise and wonderment. There he noticed a group of Yiddish writers and readers discussing Yiddish books and literature. He moved closer to them. At the sight of a policeman, the group suddenly froze in silence. Perhaps it was because they had carried away with them bitter memories from Europe where a uniform was usually identified with cruelty and oppression.

Nathan suddenly broke the ice by speaking in the vernacular, telling them that he would like to join in the discussion. Before departing from the bookshop, he learned that there were Yiddish authors who rated beside some of the greatest contemporary American literary lights.

From that day on Nathan spent his spare hours in the bookshop, each time learning more and more about the beauty and depth of Yiddish literature. The owner of the bookshop and his followers received him cordially and began to look upon him as a buddy. Speaking an idiomatic and fluent Yiddish, he began to feel like one of them.

One day when the discussion was over, Nathan casually browsed through a book of verse by Morris Rosenfeld, and it moved him deeply. He read more and more, and his interest grew by leaps and bounds. A wondrous literature was revealed to him, in many respects warmer and more intimate than English literature.

Before long Nathan purchased a set of Rosenfeld's collected works, which he read with avid interest in his home. From Rosenfeld he went to Sholem Aleichem, then to Moishe Nadir, Sholem Asch and Yossel Kotler.[14] Especially did he relish the latter author whose works are closer to him than, say, Nadir's, a writer of the same satiric genre. Being a native born American, he found Sholem Aleichem's distinctly European characters altogether foreign and remote.

So fond has Nathan become of Yiddish literature that he complains he hasn't enough time to read all the works as often as he would like. His apartment is filled with bookcases containing the works of his favorite Yiddish authors. There are also collections of works by Spencer, Mark Twain, O. Henry, Thomas Mann and Dreiser.

At the meetings of the family circle Nathan hears a cultured Yiddish spoken, and participates in the discussions. He regrets that so few American-born Jewish young men and women are aware of the creative work done in the vernacular. His own brother, for instance, a highly informed person, who had attended Hebrew schools and learned to read and write Yiddish, is totally indifferent to Yiddish literature and culture.

Besides being a policeman, Nathan is at present a father. Two years ago he married the girl of his heart and a year later their firstborn came. He established himself in a modern Brownsville apartment and not in the elegant home he once dreamed of designing. Earning $250 a month, he and his family live quite comfortably. He misses little in life except more time to read. However, he is not his own master. He must be ready for duty at a moment's notice and put in a twenty hour shift, if necessary.

And so Nathan, the would-be-designer of houses, has made the best of his opportunities. He was not beaten by the Depression, as many thousands of youths have been. He is a symbol of American adjustment to circumstances.

PART THREE

Contemporary Landslayt in New York

Continuities and Discontinuities

Since the surveys of Jewish immigrant clubs in New York City conducted over half a century ago by the WPA, the evolution of these groups has been marked by significant adaptations, as has the connotation of the concept of landslayt. The bonds of benevolence, verified by the Yiddish Writers' Group as giving meaning to associational life in the earlier part of the twentieth century, have been continually remolded. The directions taken, as landsmanshaft organizations adjust the doctrine of helping others while helping themselves, reflect the overall transformation of the ethnic enclave.

The spirit of New York Jewry in the first quarter of this century, as characterized by Arthur Goren as a community engaged in a "dual process— the struggle to maintain ethnic integrity and to achieve social accommodation,"[1] was also detected by Rontch and his colleagues in their scrutiny of landsmanshaftn and family circles just prior to World War II. The mandate "to preserve the solidarity . . . , to provide a measure of personal security . . . , [and] to fit . . . into the American social landscape"[2] continues to be a compelling challenge several generations later. It was evident in the postwar period, as landsmanshaft members learned of the destruction of European Jewry and witnessed the rise of the State of Israel.

As we have seen, landsmanshaft participants founded synagogues, provided financial assistance and medical insurance benefits, and guaranteed the right to traditional Jewish burial to member families. They actively raised funds for the upkeep of institutions in the hometown and regularly granted aid to numerous charitable causes. One other important activity which these societies undertook was the preparation of memorial books, known as yisker books. The publication of these volumes, usually prepared to honor the memory of the entire community that was destroyed during World War II, often replaced the self-help and relief functions of the landsmanshaftn, once it became clear that plans to rehabilitate the European towns were futile.[3] Naturally, the Rontch study could not have anticipated this new preoccupation.

How can we account for and interpret the pervasiveness of landsmanshaft affiliation throughout the Jewish community, among men and women of various socioeconomic classes, for the generation of children of immigrants born in America before World War I, as well as for post-World War II immigrants and their offspring? My interviews with representatives of landsmanshaftn in New York, and also Philadelphia and Tel Aviv, nearly fifty years after *Jewish Landsmanschaften and Family Circles of New York* was prepared for publication, confirm that these immigrant organizations continue to function as transmitters of both cultural continuity and change in the new country of settlement.

My update of the agendas of contemporary landsmanshaftn and their evolution involved locating a study sample and meeting with leaders of sixty-eight organizations. Yet another view of the nature and development of organizational dynamics was generated through weekly monitoring of the New York Yiddish and English-language Jewish press from January 1983 to

December 1984, as well as by surveying the Yiddish dailies for reactions to the Holocaust on the part of landsmanshaftn during the early years of World War II, from 1938 to 1941. Landsmanshaft publications were also scrutinized, and archival sources and organizational records were consulted. Taken together, these multiple strands of evidence provide rich data on landsmanshaftn as vehicles for participation in postwar America.[4]

Landsmanshaft activity peaked in the early decades of the twentieth century, when these organizations proliferated during World War I to help finance relief work in their respective birthplaces in Europe. The 1938 survey catalogued approximately two thousand associations that utilized and modified the landsmanshaft structure. Family circles were identified in this typology as the favored outgrowth of the landsmanshaft model of affiliation, as the needs and circumstances of immigrant Jews and their American-born offspring changed.

The landsmanshaft community was infused with new spirit and novel purpose when refugees from Europe joined existing societies after World War II, or else initiated new landsmanshaftn to represent their unique bond as Holocaust survivors. Their arrival also underscored the differences between them and prior waves of immigrants, particularly in their expressions of affiliation as Jews of East European descent now in America. Despite the common link to a European community of origin, the previous settlers had become distanced from the hometown. For the postwar survivors who settled in New York in the 1940s and early 1950s, their Lodz, Minsk, or Warsaw was different from the city remembered by the earlier immigrants.

In the years since the arrival of this last major influx to populate New York's immigrant clubs, the landsmanshaft sector has undoubtedly been reduced in size. Societies have disbanded, the flow of immigrants has dwindled, and the profile of the leadership has changed. Yet, despite predictions of their virtual disappearance in the second and third American-born generations, a forecast that echoes throughout the twentieth century, there are signs of landsmanshaft continuity even as we approach the twenty-first century.

Of the categories of landsmanshaft societies formulated in 1938 by the Yiddish Writers' Group of the Federal Writers' Project, each subdivision is currently represented.[5] Indeed, the accuracy and long-lived utility of Rontch's framework are almost uncanny. Of course, it is imperative to note the decrease in the absolute number of societies, especially the diminished number of branches affiliated with national orders and the dissolution of united relief organizations. However, it is just as important, and in a sense more interesting, to understand how and why the traditional community model of belonging and benevolence has been borrowed and adapted.

The original and unique purpose of an association may be retained only in its name, and not necessarily in its actual work. A landsmanshaft congregation, such as the Chevra Anshe Antopolier, may no longer be concentrated in its own synagogue center. Or, when a landsmanshaft synagogue like New York's Bialystok Synagogue does still stand, its active membership may not currently derive from the original namesake. Another change is the character of the "young men's" benevolent associations. Those that continue to meet consist largely of a senior citizen population, and women's membership is invited.

The varied contexts for participation that landsmanshaftn once provided continue to be evident in the distinctions between organizations that are sustained even today. Though many of the original founders are forgotten and the paths they intended have shifted, societies remain steadfast in their individuality as long as is feasible. Nevertheless, certain shared elements of landsmanshaft existence remain at the core of all groups. Burial arrangements, the principles of mutual aid, and social fellowship endure as central tenets of landsmanshaft life.

The primary benefit provided by landsmanshaftn that continues to attract some new members is the assurance of a proper Jewish funeral. Constitutions detail the customary procedures, the organization's obligations, and the monetary assistance distributed to the surviving spouse. Amounts which were once stipulated for these benefits hardly suffice to meet present costs, and the appointment of special committees to oversee funerals has become outdated. In earlier years, a cemetery committee would have convened monthly to supervise the allocation of plots. Today, there is more likely to be one member who is charged with this task, and who is responsible for contacting the organization's funeral parlor when informed of a death. It is not uncommon for family members and offspring who request the reservation of a cemetery plot alongside their relatives to thus be drawn to join the organization, and to express symbolically commitment to the landsmanshaft spirit of camaraderie, in life and in death.

Other mutual aid functions resurge as needed and are activated in a new manner. The medical services and sickness benefits which were a chief attraction of landsmanshaftn have been superseded by widely available insurance policies. Interest-free loans were typically offered to needy members, and special funds ensured that compatriots in America or Europe would be able to celebrate Jewish holidays festively. These practices are now refashioned to include sending this kind of relief to Israel, or assisting elderly members by suspending or reducing dues when they cannot be met.

In addition to providing monetary assistance and the services of a local doctor, early landsmanshaftn commonly appointed individuals to the role of "hospitalers." These officers acted as emissaries of the society in visiting ailing members and helping to facilitate the distribution of aid. In some organizations, this station was shared by several volunteers, with each hospitaler responsible for a different borough for the members of their sex. The office of hospitaler not only institutionalized the traditional Jewish practice of visiting the sick, but it also was a way to confirm the maladies of the potential recipient of sick benefits. While some groups still retain this position, others merely announce illnesses and recent deaths at meetings, and one officer is authorized to represent the landsmanshaft at funerals.[6]

In general, a landsmanshaft leader today must assume multiple responsibilities. The following posts, for example, were discussed at a meeting of the Czenstochauer Young Men which I attended: president, vice president, financial secretary, recording secretary, treasurer, trustees, chairmen of the cemetery and membership committees, and inner guard. Yet, one veteran member of the group remarked, after observing the difficulties in filling these positions: "There was a time when there were fights on the floor, everyone wanted to be an officer; today, people don't even want to accept nominations."[7] One solution, in such cases, is simply to abridge the roster to reflect changes in organizational structure, and thus allow the group's operation to be carried forth.

Philanthropic practices locally in New York and on behalf of the hometown communities have also undergone changes over the years. Fundraising for worthy causes, both Jewish and general, on the larger American scene is still a central purpose.[8] As for the native country, this concern has understandably been largely abandoned today. Nevertheless, some organizations still support the few Jews that remain in their European communities, or else work to maintain or refurbish Jewish cemeteries or any other monuments testifying to the prewar Jewish community that once thrived.[9] Since World War II Israel has undoubtedly been another chief recipient of landsmanshaft contributions, as prior charities have been replaced by a new concentration on the well-being of the Jewish State.[10]

It was the Second World War and the shocking destruction of Jewish life in Europe that, more than anything else, redirected the character of the landsmanshaft's focus, philanthropic and otherwise. One group's meeting notice of September 1948, written in Yiddish, lucidly illustrates the new challenges. Members were urged to attend an upcoming meeting to discuss the following issues: (1) Should we help the Jews in Israel? (2) Should we also help our landslayt in the Old Home? If so, how? (3) Should we join the central relief organization of American landslayt, or should our relief efforts be conducted independently?[11]

Since World War II concern for the native country understandably has been largely abandoned except as a focus of commemoration. Some landsmanshaftn did not even form until after 1945, prompted by appeals to aid those who had survived and to memorialize the annihilation of the hometown. Typically in this quest, the initiators corresponded with counterparts in Israel and around the world regarding their interest in publishing a yisker book to document the achievements of their community, as well as its destruction by the Nazis. The memorial books, like the news bulletins, organizational correspondence, and souvenir journals, figure as modes of communication by which individuals are reminded of their special memberships. Yet these volumes bear their own distinctive stamp in their preoccupation with history and memory.

Within the landsmanshaft, social occasions that foster friendship and a sense of alliance with a network of colleagues are the fundraising events for special projects, whether to secure funds for publication of a yisker book or to collect donations for charitable causes. The regularity of scheduled meetings has declined from the once common norm of weekly gatherings in a neighborhood hall, in some cases, to a yearly dinner at a central downtown location. On these occasions business matters are aired and a dispersed membership can reclaim its bonds. The official deliberations of the meetings are not any more important than the opportunity these get-togethers provide for companionship and communication. The unofficial agenda may, in fact, be even more significant. "What we discuss is unimportant," exclaimed one landsmanshaft leader, "as long as we get a chance to talk with one another."[12]

Of the meeting halls where Rontch and his coworkers roamed in search of landsmanshaft headquarters, the Free Sons of Israel building in lower Manhattan still retains the buzz of activity on a Sunday afternoon, hosting groups which maintain lockers filled with the documents and regalia of organizational life. In the 1930s, Rontch and his colleagues noted the tendency of some groups to meet in one of the city's hotels or restaurants. Today, societies may choose to convene in boroughs where a majority of the members presently reside.

An alternative that has been offered to landsmanshaftn in recent years is to convene at the central offices of the United Jewish Appeal in New York. When organizations consider this new option for their assemblies, the decision signifies something beyond a mere shift in location. It confirms that the group has taken an explicit turn in the direction of support for Israel, and that a measure of its own independence has been relinquished to the centralized fundraising bodies. Landsmanshaftn are recruited to join various campaigns, and they respond to solicitations on the part of the United Jewish Appeal, the Bonds for Israel, the Jewish National Fund, or the Israel Histradrut Campaign. Meetings are visited by emissaries from these agencies, and testimonial dinners hosted by these offices are occasions to raise money by honoring active members in constituent landsmanshaftn.

This shift away from hometown-oriented relief and mutual aid toward support of Israel leads to new platforms and new declarations, as present leaders retrospectively redefine the group's original precepts to match present agendas.[13] Of course, these reconstructions of organizational goals are far from the principles which the founders envisioned at the time of their society's incorporation in the early part of the century, when hardly any immigrant association was defending aid to Palestine.

The landsmanshaftn originated as hometown-based, hometown-oriented associations, but they owe their endurance in America to this very ability to constantly replace and regenerate priorities. Preservation of the group ultimately depends not on any absolute set of rules or terms of membership, but on the quality of relationships among members at different times. Connectedness with a community of people here in America outweighs the pull of a common European community of origin.

One daughter perceptively summarized the drawing power of these bonds in describing her mother's dedication to the Ladies Auxiliary of the Bialystoker Home for the Aged. It was not her birth in Bialystok, but "the feeling for people" and the fact that participation in the organization provided a network of friends and "was a way of getting together." Furthermore, it is clearer today than ever that ties to Bialystok and its institutions are not the sole criteria for membership in the Ladies Auxiliary. Typically, those who join are women who live in the neighborhood of the Bialystoker Home, who are attracted to the social events and charity work of the group. In the context of this American-born daughter's own lifelong involvement in the same society that had attracted her mother's volunteer spirit, it is not surprising that this development is viewed with mixed sentiments. The fact that "they don't have the feeling we do, they're not Bialystoker . . . ," she states somewhat equivocally, "doesn't mean they cannot be involved in an organization."[14]

It is not uncommon to find that societies no longer restrict landslayt status only to fellow townspeople. One delegate from the Lodz branch of her fraternal order, the Workmen's Circle, claims: "they take in every member . . . because they need the people." New candidates are not placed in branches that are geographically connected to their origins in Europe, but rather their application assigns them to a branch in New York that is geographically convenient for their travel in the city. And yet, "people don't want to be wiped out entirely," and request the retention of their town name when a merger of several smaller branches occurs.[15]

Even in earlier years, according to the 1938 WPA survey, nonlandslayt relatives and friends were welcomed into the landsmanshaft. What, if not rootedness in a shared birthplace, is the allure of the landsmanshaft? And who are the people involved in the modern-day landsmanshaftn?

A sense of personal obligation, "a kind of trust that was handed down," motivates some leaders to continue the family traditions of landsmanshaft activism.[16] Others who persevere in doing the necessary and often thankless tasks that keep an organization alive acknowledge that nostalgia is an underlying motive for their work in building community in the setting of the landsmanshaft.

In the second half of the twentieth century, landsmanshaft leaders in New York City include those in their thirties who inherited the task of recordkeeping from their fathers, such as the son of the rabbi of the First Warschauer Congregation who supervised this synagogue-based landsmanshaft after his father's death until the sale of the building and ultimate dissolution of the group.[17] One of my oldest informants was the president and caretaker of the Congregation Czenstochauer Chasam Sopher. This edifice, located in New York's Lower East Side, still stands. However, this locality-based immigrant synagogue no longer services members from the designated place name, Czestochowa, as it once did when settlers from that city lived in the vicinity, and the European place name has been virtually expunged.

Most interviewees were men, but I found women represented in ladies' auxiliaries, in their own ladies' aid societies, and also in organizations that once served a male constituency but which today welcome spouses as full-fledged members. Whatever their official capacity, women deservedly earn the distinction of being the true keepers of landsmanshaft lore. Over and over, I encountered women who were more knowledgeable than their husbands about the association and whose family ties were more authentic and went back further historically. A son-in-law, it turns out, would typically be recruited into the landsmanshaft upon marriage. His own family genealogy was discounted, and the young American-born grooms became prime candidates for climbing the leadership scale to positions of power.

In America the landsmanshaft has expanded its boundaries to include spouses, relatives, and friends who supplement the original core of male immigrants originating from the same birthplace. Guild-like landsmanshaftn such as the Bialystoker Bricklayers, the Bialystoker Operators Club, the Bialystoker Painters, and the Bialystoker Cutters Social Club welcomed landslayt with shared occupational status. Landsmanshaft divisions of national fraternities such as the Workmen's Circle or the International Workers' Order served the needs of immigrant laborers. The socioeconomic demographics that characterize the landsmanshaft sector today map a more diversified population than indicated by Rontch's statistics, including accountants, store owners, housewives, lawyers, bookkeepers, executives, and stockbrokers.

In general, the discernible patterns in the development of landsmanshaft identity that we have traced show how Jewish immigrant associations in the United States demonstrate the emergence of new forms of ethnic affiliation which develop as a means of social adjustment to new conditions. In his study of the Jewish family circle, a kindred structure to the landsmanshaft, as Rontch had emphasized, William Mitchell underscored this adaptive quality of the system of relationships which voluntary associations embody. He argued that the supportive web of family interaction available to the membership was meaningful at different times for emotional sustenance, economic assistance, or sociality and solidarity. Mitchell posited that these functions were variously prominent at different junctures in the life of each group and in the life of each participant. The total complex of multiple benefits that was ready for members to appeal to within the framework of their club made participation attractive and viable.[18] Sklare notes the resilience of these groups in demonstrating both an ability to remain responsive to changing needs, and "an abiding desire to continue kinship bonds."[19] The family circle, like the landsmanshaft, achieved bonding through accommodation.

Modifications of the landsmanshaft model of affiliation emerge as the circumstances of immigrant Jews and their American-born children take a new turn. For example, the membership is no longer delimited solely by geography, Yiddish is replaced by English as the primary language of communication, and responses to issues and events change. Since the study conducted by the Federal Writers' Project Yiddish Writers' Group, the evolutionary nature of landsmanshaft interests is most strikingly evident in the shift in focus from hometown to homeland. Within the boundary of the landsmanshaft community, members struggle to integrate their different concerns—allegiance to their East European origins, support for Israel, participation as American citizens. I found many longstanding leaders eager to declare their Americanness and, thereby, their puzzlement as to how they could be of help in my study. Their declaration, "but I'm not from the other side," was offered simultaneously with an explanation for their motivation to join the landsmanshaft and continue as active members, namely "I *am* an Antopoler" or "my parents are from Bialystok."

This unresolved ambivalence finds expression in many spheres, with one or the other alliance articulated more strikingly at different times. In years past, the decision-making process regarding aid to the European hometown reflected the pulls of multiple attachments; today the pivotal relationship of the group to American society has similarly been transferred onto the deliberations to determine the place Israel should assume in the mission of the organization. Despite their vigorous support of Israel, for example, there are American leaders who have never visited Israel, and there is not a particularly strong alliance with Israeli landslayt. In fact, generalized giving to Israel supersedes any sense of personal responsibility for the Israeli landsmanshaft affiliate.

The intricacy of landsmanshaft loyalties reflects the complexity of the overlapping of three generations of members—the immigrants themselves, their children, and their grandchildren. Moreover, there is not a direct correspondence between age and distance from the immigration experience. Veteran landsmanshaft leaders may well have been born in America, and their non-immigrant position is what many of them emphasize. The point is that the attachment and affinity seemingly fostered by the landsmanshaft with the "old world" were means to an end: adjustment to the new land. The process of acculturation was paradoxically eased and even advanced as an outcome of these bonds. The associations' priorities, in other words, are shaped by the society in which the group presently resides.

The ways in which the declaration of affiliation with the hometown emerges in the new country of settlement are perhaps best highlighted by focusing on a period of time that tests landsmanshaft links to the old and the new home, the early years of World War II. For the years between 1939 and

1941, a period which I hypothesized to be a critical time to judge whether landsmanshaftn were predisposed more than the rest of the community to exhibit special awareness about the situation of European Jewry, I examined the relationship between the media and the landsmanshaftn in order to learn about the availability of sources for news and for guidance on the course of action to be pursued in response to the war.

Studies of the press during the Nazi reign which attempt to decipher the American public's reaction to the Holocaust note the relative inattention to the impending annihilation of European Jewry. One observer, Haskell Look-stein, views the Yiddish press in particular as a "major source of Jewish news . . . which provided virtually a measurement of the pulse of the community," its values, and its norms.[20] Do the assessments of these researchers hold for landsmanshaft members, and how did the Yiddish press communicate reports and directives to this sector concerning the events of World War II?

According to my survey, during the initial years before the United States entered the war, appeals for unity appeared intermittently in the Yiddish dailies, the main public outlet for the landsmanshaftn. If we sample the articles on landsmanshaft activities in *The Day* throughout the duration of the interval in question, we find discussions of standard organizational affairs and conventional issues.[21] On the other hand, there are some indications during these years that the times were not ordinary ones, as headlines urged landsmanshaftn to reconsider their fundraising work on behalf of the old home and to renew their aid on a broader scale by revitalizing the landsmanshaft federations that had functioned as relief agencies during World War I. However, the dominant concern was preparation for the work of reconstructing Europe at the eventual end of the war.

My survey of the Yiddish press for the years 1939 to 1941 suggests that the unexpected disengagement of the landsmanshaftn was conditioned by the reduced identification of their members with their respective places of origin and their acclimatization to their new society. Indeed, when organizations did mobilize, their work mainly supported the American military effort, and in general their activities paralleled the response of the country as a whole.

There is evidence of detachment even in earlier years when immigrants had only recently arrived from their native Russia or Poland. The older immigrant leaders were viewed as "very American" by the second generation heirs to these positions.[22] In a souvenir journal of the Lodzer Young Men's Benevolent Society, for example, members proposed to change the name of the organization to U.S. Lodge of the Young Men's Benevolent Society, arguing that the once magical word Lodz would "discourage those who follow us from taking our places in the organization in future years."[23] The proposal to choose a name not linked to the birthplace of its members did not prevail. But the debate itself powerfully symbolized the process of dissociation that became more visible both during and after World War II.

As for the younger American-born leaders of today's organizations, they may not necessarily know the geographical dimensions or historical legacy of the communities their societies represent. One of the six sites whose landsmanshaftn I studied, the major urban center of Lodz, was mistakenly referred to as a small town, a shtetl, by second and third generation members.

In the case of Lodz landsmanshaftn in New York, a group of survivors from the city elected to join the existing Lodzer Young Men's Benevolent Society, but initially remained a separate faction. Yet another organization of Lodz landslayt who chose to recall their home in Lodz only in terms of their incarceration in the Lodz Ghetto during World War II have named their independent society accordingly. For others, Lodz is remembered for its religious Orthodox community, whose commemoration and preservation is the basis for a separate association.

The various characteristics that I have delineated for the study population as a whole are highlighted in a more focused portrait of Bialystok landsmanshaftn. The public work of the Bialystok affiliates in New York is coordinated by the Bialystoker Center, which represents the legacy of Bialystok Jewry to the community at large. The center reminds its group and individual members of their obligations to the upkeep of the Bialystoker Home and Infirmary for the Aged and to the center.

The director of the Bialystoker Center is a full-time employee who manages affairs related to the center's maintenance as a symbolic home for Bialystok descendants the world over. He also orchestrates various events that bring together representatives of the Bialystoker landsmanshaftn and Center supporters. The Center disburses charitable donations to various U.S. and Israeli causes, as well as any aid to the city of Bialystok. It also distributes the Yiddish-English journal, *Bialystoker Shtimme* [*Voice of Bialystok*] worldwide.

The Center's current leaders are mainly Holocaust survivors who organized a Bialystoker Friends club in 1945 as a division of the Center. Today, the activities of this subgroup—for example, convening Holocaust commemoration assemblies or perpetuating the cultural accomplishments of pre-war Jewish Bialystok—now dominate the Center's programming and its publications.[24]

The occupational requisites once necessary for subgroups seeking membership in the Bialystoker landsmanshaft are evident in the titles of such groups as the Bialystoker Bricklayers Benevolent Association. Today, the offspring of the laborers who founded this landsmanshaft continue the tradition of affiliation, mainly through occasional meetings at the center and regular participation in concerts and dinners hosted by the Bialystoker Center.[25]

Another occupation group, the Bialystoker Cutters Social Club, welcomed Bialystok descendants working as cutters in New York's garment industry. However, the club also included others who enrolled for recreation and for the company of friends, irrespective of Bialystok origins. In fact, when the Club earmarked contributions to the Bialystoker Center, the United Jewish Appeal, and HIAS, Boys' Town also received support at the suggestion of several non-Jewish members, Italian garment workers, who had joined the league.[26]

Restrictions on membership in the Bialystok Ladies Auxiliary have also loosened. Still open only to women, this group actively supports the Bialystoker Home. However, the general membership no longer exhibits any special attachment to Bialystok; rather, women who live near the center join because they enjoy the social functions. Leaders I interviewed, who remember the devotion of the parent generation, regarded this development as both regrettable and inevitable. Yet, because of their willingness not to circumscribe the criteria for membership, at a time when other organizations are threatened by the possibility of disbanding, groups like the Bialystoker Ladies Auxiliary continue to meet weekly. Founded in 1923, the Bialystoker Ladies Auxiliary switched to biweekly luncheons only in the mid-1980s, when the two chief officers felt overtaxed by their other organizational obligations.

For some members the landsmanshaft is their sole organizational venture. However, as in the case of the Bialystoker Ladies' representatives, it is not at all uncommon for landsmanshaft members to have multiple affiliations and to assume multiple leadership roles. Women may be involved in Hadassah, Pioneer Women, or the synagogue sisterhood; men may be active in the Masons or the Knights of Pythias.

The neighborhood around the Bialystoker Center also supports another institution that still functions under the Bialystok name. The Bialystoker Synagogue, among the oldest synagogues on New York's Lower East Side, was originally founded by Jews from Bialystok. Although the synagogue maintains friendly if minimal relations with the Bialystoker Center, the rabbi and congregation have no connection with the ancestral home. Yet there is no thought of changing the name.[27]

Another reminder of the older traditions of Bialystok landsmanshaft life is the Bialystoker Unterstitzungs Verein Somach Noflim, founded in 1886. At the time of my fieldwork, this group's officer still lived in the primary neighborhood of first settlement, in fact adjacent to the Bialystoker Center.[28] A copy of the *Bialystoker Shtimme* he had received remained unopened, because he disapproved of the photographs of immodest females in sleeveless shirts and males without the headcovering required by orthodox Jews. His alienation was intensified by the periodical's news about unfamiliar newcomers, for whom the Somach Noflim is a relic of the past.

Another enduring group, dating from 1906, is the Bialystoker Young Men's Association. The Young Men's officer fondly remembered his tenure in the organization as "a good training ground" for mastering the rules of political life, which eventually prepared him for his career choice as a lawyer.[29] In general, this was the type of organization that appealed to the middle-class values of the sons and sons-in-law engaged in training for professional endeavors.

Fidelity to labor causes and to the dignity of the working class is paired with regional loyalty in the Workmen's Circle Bialystok Branch 88. This landsmanshaft's Yiddish journal, *Bialystoker Friend,* discusses matters of special concern to those for whom being Workmen's Circle members and Bialystoker landslayt are inseparable. Another national fraternal order, the Farband Labor Zionist Alliance, once also supported a separate Bialystok division; however only the historical records hint at a once vibrant collaboration.[30]

An active partnership does exist between the Bialystoker Center and the American Gathering of Jewish Holocaust Survivors. The pages of the *Shtimme* detail the participation of center delegates at the conventions held by the American Gathering, such as the one held in Philadelphia in 1985. The attendance of the Gathering's president at a recent Holocaust remembrance ceremony organized by the center is seen as symbolic of the reciprocal bonds.

In the 1990s Bialystok landsmanshaft activity is not as varied as in 1938 or 1908, but it remains a persistent aspect of American Jewish communal life. Landsmanshaftn do not merely provide a setting for leisure time pursuits, although this function is a crucial one, nor can the dispensation of material benefits be considered of prime importance. My fieldwork in New York City has shown that the way in which landsmanshaftn orient themselves as an ethnic unit reflects their position in American society today, which is certainly different from the social milieu in which they were situated when the WPA study was initiated. The once stricter interpretation of the landsmanshaft as a gathering of fellow townspeople has been modified. Will it widen still further to encompass acceptance of the term landslayt as a designation for fellow Jews in general?

Many present landsmanshaft leaders perceive the future of their organizations in a way that devalues the link to a common birthplace or residence in Eastern Europe. Indeed, many landsmanshaft activists are pessimistic about the viability of this form of organization. In this respect, my expression of interest in their organization was often met with surprise. Rontch and the Yiddish Writers' Group of the Federal Writers' Project of New York encountered the same demurral, even consternation.

But that is beside the point. Despite predictions of the disappearance of landsmanshaft societies and periodic public forecasts that bemoan the predicament of Jewish survival overall, my work points to the resolute tenacity of individuals and groups in finding means for expressing their position as Jews within American society. The tension of being caught between the two worlds of Eastern Europe and the United States has had creative consequences for the continuity of Jewish community life in this country. The remarkable legacy of the extraordinary flourishing of grassroots organization and leadership which the Yiddish Writers' Group uncovered is still apparent in the profile of the American Jewish community today.

The Yiddish press, the in-house journals, and the organizational records are available for study at the Yivo Institute for Jewish Research, the American Jewish Historical Society, the American Jewish Archives, the Diaspora Research Institute in Tel Aviv, and numerous other repositories, including private collections stored away in attics. The insights and memories of participants in this world are still accessible. By integrating interview data with archival materials, and through the venturesome utilization of primary sources to validate personal reminiscences, my research has successfully challenged the thesis that landsmanshaftn claimed only those individuals doomed to remain stagnant in their steadfast loyalty to a world left behind.

In the United States, East European Jews organized society after society to help them adjust to their new homes. These organizations helped immigrants cope with life in the new country of settlement and, in turn, the associations were destined to be shaped by the immigrants' accommodation to the larger society. In the framework of their hometown clubs, members explored the changing meaning of their ethnicity. The flexible structure of these associations ensures the continuity of Jewish organizational dynamics and Jewish life in new settings.

BIBLIOGRAPHIC GUIDE

When the Yiddish Writers' Group of the New York City branch of the Federal Writers' Project embarked on their study of Jewish immigrant associations in the 1930s, they noted the lack of a systematic body of research to steer them along their path. While this situation is now somewhat improved, and there are available bibliographic tools, they must be ferreted out from among a variety of disciplinary literatures and vantage points. Taken together, these different yet interrelated components help to prepare the way for thinking about Jewish voluntary associations as expressions of ethnic identification in pluralist societies.

An informed discussion of multiculturalism in America must begin by considering a view of this country by Milton Gordon as "a 'multi-structural' society with some cultural diversity, rather than a melting pot."[1] From this vantage point, which recognizes that ethnic group life is shaped by the ongoing transmission of strategies for negotiating the dominant mainstream culture, the search can proceed for what Peggy Reeves Sanday calls "a way of looking at the options open to an individual" in a culturally diverse society like the United States.[2] One important consequence of this outlook on ethnicity is that it directs our attention to the internal social organization of immigrant-based communities to help elucidate the different ways in which individuals become American. For the immigrant, institutions such as the ethnic voluntary association serve, for W. I. Thomas, "either to interpret the new or to hold him steady while he is getting adjusted."[3]

Immigrant clubs represent one sort of agency formed by nationality groups to facilitate their transition in the new, usually urban environment, while preserving their own culture.[4] A wider perspective on the role of voluntary associations in history is presented in an overview by Constance Smith and Anne Freedman.[5] Robert T. Anderson suggests that these organizations always existed as adaptive mechanisms to support individuals in situations of social change.[6] He suggests, furthermore, that "voluntary associations may play a special role for migrants," citing examples from the anthropological literature that show how "migrants transplant, in this way, traditional institutions to foreign soil."[7]

In the United States, a long history of fraternal beneficiary societies predates the relatively recent interest in the motivations and consequences of entry into these networks.[8] William Kornhauser's theory of mass society and democratic order initiated the specification of how voluntary associations act as intermediary structures that link the individual and society's political elite.[9] The fleshing out of this theory of mediating collectivities remained the task of ensuing investigations, attempting to describe and explain differences among associations as well as between joiners and nonmembers.[10] The evidence, to date, writes David Knoke, "points almost uniformly to favorable personal consequences for members."[11]

Voluntary associations, in general, have been envisaged by Ferdinand Tonnies and W. Lloyd Warner as counterweights to the spread of modern city life.[12] In the U.S. metropolis, feared to be steadily undermining the interconnections of its citizens, urban social networks are found by Edward O. Laumann to persist, including the formal and informal associations of ethnic minority members.[13] These findings have been confirmed for more recent waves of newcomers in works by Nancy Foner and Shirley Jenkins.[14]

In a collection on the behaviors and institutions of various ethnic groups in the city of Detroit, edited by O. Feinstein, the associational involvements of immigrants were found to reflect the fact that "no ethnic minority group, including a predominantly immigrant one, is homogeneous and undifferentiated."[15] In his discussion of nineteenth-century Chinese associations established in San Francisco's Chinatown, Stanford M. Lyman similarly reasons that interassociational power struggles between clans reproduce factionalism and status conflicts in the native land.[16] Ethnic voluntary associations are said by Djuro J. Vrga to incorporate the "adjustment of successive immigrations to each other and . . . the adjustment of each immigration to the host society."[17] This model concurs with other work in non-U.S. settings.[18]

Pre-immigration experiences influence the structure and dynamics of ethnic group life in the new home, yet the ethnic enclave is not merely a re-creation of community in the region of origin. According to John Bodnar, ethnicity is not "simply part of the cultural baggage of the immigrant. It was also a product of the immigrant communities established in America . . . ," thereby marked by diversity and division.[19] The impetus to multiplication and elaboration of organizations applies to the development in the United States of numerous voluntary hometown-based associations, not only for Jewish immigrants, but also including those serving Slavic, Greek, Filipino, Japanese, and Italian immigrants.[20]

Richard N. Juliani's research on the immigration of Italians to Philadelphia is particularly insightful in terms of parallels for the Jewish experience of an analysis of how "not a single, monolithic community, but rather an elaborate varied proliferation of 'little Italies' existed, based upon specific loyalties to hometown friends and relatives." The resultant profusion of voluntary *societe,* based on this principle of village, or *paesani,* relationships created a situation where "even very small towns could have had several societies in Philadelphia, reflecting opposing factions . . . or due to ambitious leaders who wanted power."[21] As the Italian community evolved, regional hostilities and conflicts were overwhelmed by new self-identities emanating from the American milieu. Ironically, Juliani points out, in becoming Americanized, immigrants also became Italian, such that "*paesano* is used, by the younger generation, for any other person of Italian descent."[22] The term landslayt, I would hypothesize, may well encounter a similar fate.

These stages and manifestations of ethnic group identification have been characterized more generally, by Jonathan Sarna, as the advancement of "ethnicization."[23] Won Moo Hurh outlines the process, reasoning from the Korean-American experience, as a progression that "begins with contacts among . . . immigrants who share a feeling of being happy to see fellow-countrymen in a strange land," followed by more specific attraction to "someone from their home provinces," until "intra-group competition intensifies." As a collective awareness of their marginality grows, compatriots eventually rediscover their commonalities and reconnect in ways that no longer mandate regional affiliation.[24]

In the literature on ethnic voluntary associations and the natural path of ethnic group association, theoretical and methodological considerations which bear directly upon the study of landsmanshaftn are presented by Helena Lopata, who updated and extended the work of W. I. Thomas and Florian Znaniecki on Polish migration by surveying the membership and leaders of twenty voluntary associations in Chicago's Polonia community.[25] She also depicted how the Polish media "helped Polish-American associations . . . as a whole to develop, crystallize, and even change their basic orientation,"[26] concluding that regular reporting on voluntary association activities casts the ethnic press as a platform for the public expression of community values and goals.

The consequences of this practice became evident with the arrival of new refugees and displaced persons from Poland immediately after World War II. They, who had

> made the old emigration and descendants realize how much they had already acculturated . . . began a process of 'educating' Polonia through the development of new activities and through the press . . . laying foundations for current attitudes.[27]

This development is seen against the finding that during World War II, in general, "there was much less direct involvement in helping Poland than there was during World War I, reflecting Polonia's Americanization."[28] Many groups in this country, especially during and after World War II, were forced to assess their relationship and responsibility to their European hometown communities, as I have shown for the sample of New York landsmanshaftn which I studied.

To date, little of the research on the landsmanshaft sector of the American Jewish community extends beyond brief descriptive accounts.[29] In 1959, Isaac Levitats had recognized the need for "gathering information . . . to launch a nationwide search for organizational materials . . . that emanate from the various associations," and proclaimed that "associational activities have hardly been treated."[30] Several master's essays contributed to the field, as did William E. Mitchell's anthropological analysis of Jewish family clubs, and Michael R. Weisser's limited attempt to describe the landsmanshaft world.[31] However, Maxwell Whiteman reminds us that what the immigrants themselves thought had yet to be unearthed, for in the main "their views were shared privately with a *landsman* over a glass of tea."[32]

The views of the landslayt of New York's Jewish immigrant associations are reflected in the publications of the Yiddish Writers' Group of the Federal Writers' Project of the WPA. The heterogeneity which existed within the Jewish immigrant community is apparent from the data, and the different types of landsmanshaft bodies which the WPA study outlined reveal the stages through which the Jewish immigrant had passed by the late 1930s. My own fieldwork and archival research, fifty years later, indicates that these voluntary associations have preserved their role as forums in which a wide variety of ethnic expression may be displayed.

Although landsmanshaftn have recently been declared the most innovative of the immigrant Jewish experiments,[33] they have not been properly represented in assessments of Jewish life in the United States. To be sure, a growing literature on American Jewish social history concentrates on patterns of change among the vast majority of people, rather than an emphasis on the public statements of the elite, in order to reconstruct patterns in the life cycle of individuals as linked to the institutions to which they belonged.[34] Yet, the vitality of landsmanshaftn in the past and the viability of the landsmanshaft model of association today has not been adequately addressed in these contexts.

The present availability of landsmanshaft materials makes it possible to approach the study of people whose life experiences have long been neglected. The range of primary sources available to researchers includes: certificates of incorporation, charters, constitutions, and other legal documents; records of membership, meetings, committees, and organizational transactions; bulletins, anniversary albums, correspondence, and photographs. In addition, the Yiddish press and the Anglo-Jewish media provide documentation on landsmanshaft activities and trends. Apart from newspapers widely circulated among themselves and to compatriots in Israel and around the world, American landsmanshaft members also produced and distributed in-house journals and assorted publications.

Even less is known about Israeli immigrant associations than about those in the United States, despite the existence of numerous Israeli immigrant federations, including a central office for Polish landsmanshaftn, headquartered in Tel Aviv and serving approximately 150 registered organizations out of an estimated 250 existing landsmanshaftn.[35] My study of contemporary landsmanshaftn in New York incorporated corresponding data on the current status of ethnic voluntary associations in Israel. Jewish immigrant associations in other countries have been explored, but a systematic comparative analysis has yet to be done.[36]

Rontch and his colleagues would probably have called for this kind of investigation, had the Federal Writers' Project continued on a healthier course. They did not envision their project, the English publication of *The Jewish Landsmanschaften and Family Circles in New York*, as their last.

APPENDIX

The Jewish Landsmanschaften of New York

PREPARED BY THE YIDDISH WRITERS'
GROUP OF THE FEDERAL WRITERS' PROJECT

WORKS PROGRESS ADMINISTRATION
IN THE CITY OF NEW YORK

Published by the
I. L. PERETZ YIDDISH WRITERS' UNION
New York, 1938

Title page and table of contents from *Di yidishe lands-manshaftn fun nyu york* (The Jewish Landsmanshaftn of New York) (New York: Federal Writers' Project, 1938).

EDITORIAL STAFF
For the Racial Group Survey:

GORDON KINGMAN
Assistant Chief Project Supervisor

ISAAC E. RONTCH
Editor, Assistant Project Supervisor

Abe Abramowitz
Max Bassin
Martin Birnbaum
Morris Blechman
Yosl Cohen
Samuel Daixel
George H. Garvin
Sol Gimplin
Boris Glassman
Eliezer Greenberg

Albert Gurio
Joseph Kaluschiner
David Kasher
Anna Richter
Sam Schwartz
Lamed Shapiro
Menashe Vaxer
Emanuel Verschleiser
Baruch A. Weinrebe (B. Rivkin)
Bernard Weinstein
Ab. Yudin

CONTENTS

Photographs by the W.P.A. Federal Art Project

JEWISH FAMILIES

AND

FAMILY CIRCLES
OF NEW YORK

BY THE

YIDDISH WRITERS' GROUP

OF THE

FEDERAL WRITERS' PROJECT

Work Projects Administration
in the City of New York

Published by the

YIDDISH WRITERS' UNION
New York, 1939

Title page and table of contents from *Yidishe familyes
un familye-krayzn fun nyu york* (Jewish Families and
Family Circles of New York) (New York: Federal Writers' Project, 1939).

FOR THE FEDERAL WRITERS' PROJECT

Managing Supervisor in Charge: Carl Malmberg.

Editor: I. E. Rontch.

Staff: A. Abramowitz, M. Bassin, M. Birnbaum, Y. Cohen, S. Daixel, G. H. Garvin, S. Gimplin, E. Greenberg, A. Gurio, Rachel Hirshkan, J. L. Kalushiner, D. Kasher, J. Katz, Lamed Shapiro, M. Vaxer, B. A. Weinrebe (B. Rivkin), B. Weinstein, A. Yudin, Lillian Zahn.

CONTENTS

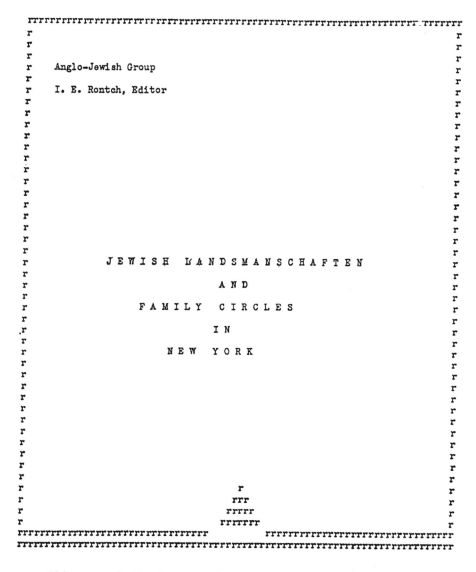

Anglo-Jewish Group

I. E. Rontch, Editor

JEWISH LANDSMANSCHAFTEN

AND

FAMILY CIRCLES

IN

NEW YORK

Title page and table of contents from an unpublished manuscript, *Jewish Landsmanschaften and Family Circles in New York.*

CONTENTS

Preface

PART ONE
Jewish Landsmanschaften

PART TWO
Family Circles

in the life of the east European Jew. Holidays as occasions for family reunions and festivities. The sanctity of marriage and family life. The high regard for Talmudic scholarship, superseding material wealth. The rise of the Haskala (renaissance) movement in the 80's and 90's of the last century. The revolt against patriarchal tyranny and traditionalism. The break between the older and younger generation and the split in the patriarchal family.

14 pages.

2. Jewish Family Circles. Newest form of mutual aid societies. The cemetery plot as the nucleus of family circles. Their rise and growth. Statistics on membership; proportion of workers, business-men and professionals. Different types of family circles. Anniversary journals. A detailed account of one of the largest family circles. Study furnishes a cross-section of the life of the typical Jewish-American middle class family.

15 pages.

Tables

3. Jewish Family Life in New York City.
   A. Economic status: causes leading to emigration from the old country. Early struggles in this country. Sweatshops, long hours, small wages. Drifting from one vocation to another in order to better one's lot. The effect of the depression. Statistics on size of families, earnings and housing. The economic status of the American-born youth. Type of vocations adopted by it as compared with the older generation. The problem of unemployment due to hard times and racial prejudice.
   B. Cultural status: lack of secular education in the old country due to poverty. Sweatshop with its long hours and small wages accountable for lack of cultural development of the older generation in this country. Type of reading and recreational activities pursued by the older generation. The cultural status of the younger generation. The lack of interest in things Jewish. Its mode of recreation as compared with the older generation.

33 pages.

4. Three Generations. Personality sketches.
   (1) Neschke, mother of eight sons. The poverty surrounding her girlhood and married life. Her love for things beautiful. Her home constantly surrounded by flowers and floral decorations. Her pogrom experiences. Loss of two children as a result of the outbreak. Her immigration to America and her subsequent peaceful life here. Death of her husband. Her old age.
   (2) Isidor, the second generation. His early poverty. Immigration to this country. Adaptation to new surroundings. How he made good, then was wiped out completely during the depression. How he managed to get back to economic security and social standing.
   (3) Nathan, the policeman. How he happened to choose his vocation. His interest in Yiddish literature and how he acquired it.

38 pages.

Appendix
   (1) Glossary   20 pages.
   (2) Directory of Jewish organizations in New York   40 pages.
   (3) Index   20 pages.

Total number of pages approximately 300 including 15 illustrations.

NOTES

Preface

1. Estimates of how many such organizations were created are imprecise because the available sources are generally undervalued by their keepers and overlooked by researchers. Community surveys conducted in New York produced divergent counts of mutual aid societies in the city, some as high as 10,000. See, for example, the New York Kehilla's *Jewish Communal Register of New York City 1917–1918* (New York: Lipshitz Press, 1918); *List of Members of Jewish Communal Institutions in New York* (New York: Council of Jewish Communal Institutions, 1914).

2. Federal Writers' Project, *Di yidishe landsmanshaftn fun nyu york* (The Jewish landsmanshaftn of New York) (New York: Yiddish Writers' Union, 1938); Federal Writers' Project, *Yidishe familyes un familye krayzn fun nyu york* (Jewish families and family circles of New York) (New York: Yiddish Writers' Union, 1939).

3. Maurice J. Karpf, *Jewish Community Organization in the United States* (New York: Bloch Publishing Co., 1938), p. 131.

4. Ibid., p. 132.

5. Isaac E. Ronch, "The Story of the Family Circle Book," typewritten manuscript, Ronch Miscellaneous File, American Jewish Archives, Cincinnati, pp. 159–60. See also Isaac E. Ronch, "The WPA Yiddish Writers Project," *Jewish Currents* 29, no. 8 (September 1975): 8–12. I have maintained the transcription of Rontch's name as it appears in the WPA publications, except when an alternate spelling is used, as in the titles above.

6. I. E. Rontch, "The Present State of the Landsmanschaften," *The Jewish Social Service Quarterly* 15, no. 4 (June 1939): 360–78.

7. Ann Banks, *First-Person America* (New York: Alfred A. Knopf, 1980), p. xiii.

8. Ibid., p. xiv.

9. Daniel M. Fox, "The Achievement of the Federal Writers' Project," *American Quarterly* 13, no. 1 (Spring 1961): 3.

10. Alfred Haworth Jones, "The Search for a Usable Past in the New Deal Era," *American Quarterly* 23, no. 5 (December 1971): 274.

11. Ann Banks and Robert Carter, *Survey of Federal Writers' Project Manuscript Holdings in State Depositories* (Washington, D.C.: American Historical Association, 1985); Katherine Davidson, *Records of the Federal Writers' Project, Work Projects Administration 1935–44* (Washington, D.C.: National Archives, 1953).

12. Jerre Mangione, *The Dream and the Deal: The Federal Writers' Project, 1935–43* (Boston: Little, Brown and Company, 1972); Monty Noam Penkower, *The Federal Writers' Project: A Study in Government Patronage of the Arts* (Urbana: University of Illinois Press, 1977).

13. My thanks to Kenneth R. Cobb, Deputy Director of the Municipal Archives of the City of New York, and to his staff for facilitating my use of these records.

Part One

1. *The Day,* 5 January 1939, p. 8.

2. See I. Shmulewitz, ed., *The Bialystoker Memorial Book* (New York: The Bialystoker Center, 1982).

3. This typology of landsmanshaft bodies is summarized in Rontch, "The Present State of the Landsmanschaften," pp. 364–69.

4. Henry Radecki, *Ethnic Organizational Dynamics: The Polish Group in Canada* (Waterloo: Wilfred Laurier University Press, 1979).

5. Rontch, "The Present State of the Landsmanschaften," p. 362.

6. Ibid., p. 361.

7. Ibid., pp. 362–64.

8. Ronch, "The Story of the Family Circle Book," p. 152. Subsequently, a letter was sent to all members of the Pam-Flicker Bialystoker Family Society by the circle's president, confirming the upcoming visits of representatives from the Yiddish Writers' Group and asking the membership to extend their full cooperation. See Harry Waterman to [Pam-Flicker Family Society], 6 October 1938, WPA Historical Records Survey, Box 3626, Municipal Archives, New York City.

9. Ronch, "The Story of the Family Circle Book," p. 153.

10. Federal Writers' Project, *The Italians of New York: A Survey* (New York: Random House, 1938), pp. v–vi.

11. Ronch, "The Story of the Family Circle Book," pp. 153–54.

12. Philip Rahv and Lillian Zahn are designated as the translators of specific Yiddish chapters in the Federal Writers' Project Records on deposit in the Manuscript Division of the Library of Congress, Washington, D.C., File A752. In addition to these two project workers, an assortment of writers, translators, and editors is named in Box 3628 and 3629 of the City of New York's Municipal Archives collection. Nathan Ausubel and Nathan Asch are also identified as contributors in Penkower, *The Federal Writers' Project*, p. 69.

13. Isaac and Elke Rontch graciously invited me to their home in November 1984. We subsequently maintained a correspondence, and I returned to Los Angeles and visited Elke Rontch in April 1989.

14. Isaac Rontch to Jacob Marcus, 10 December 1979, Ronch Miscellaneous File, American Jewish Archives, Cincinnati. The absence of any additional chapters from the manuscript was confirmed in a letter to me from Fannie Zelcer, archivist at the American Jewish Archives.

15. Ronch, "The WPA Yiddish Writers Project."

16. Isaac Rontch to Donald Thompson, 12 April 1938, File A752, Federal Writers' Project Records, Manuscript Division, Library of Congress. Dovid Katz confirmed (personal communication, 11 December 1989) that other Yiddish authors, including his father, Mienke Katz, were employed by the WPA, however not in the Writers' Project.

17. All of the project's subgroups, including the Yiddish Writers' Group, had to locate their own patrons to support publication costs and to aid in distribution. See Yiddish Writers' Union collection, Record Group 701, Yivo Institute for Jewish Research, New York City.

18. Ronch, "The WPA Yiddish Writers Project," p. 8.

19. See Yiddish Writers' Group of the Federal Writers' Project to the I. L. Peretz Yiddish Writers' Union, 15 November 1938, File 262, Record Group 701, Yivo Institute for Jewish Research, New York City.

20. Ronch, "The WPA Yiddish Writers Project," p. 10.

21. Ibid., pp. 11–12. The suspicions of the Dies Committee about the Communist predilections of the Federal Writers' Project are discussed in Mangione, *The Dream and the Deal*, pp. 289–328, and Penkower, *The Federal Writers' Project*, pp. 194–200.

22. Ronch, "The WPA Yiddish Writers Project," p. 11.

23. The popularity of the book is attested to by Mangione, *The Dream and the Deal*, p. 277. Also, requests for copies came not only from local readers, but also from Europe, according to book orders found in the WPA Historical Records Survey, Box 3626, Municipal Archives, New York City.

24. Ronch, "The Story of the Family Circle Book," p. 156.

25. Ibid. Subsequently, B. Hoffman, president of the Yiddish Writers' Union, confirmed the approval of the union in sponsoring publication of the manuscript. See B. Hoffman to Carl Malmberg, 3 July 1939, File 260, Record Group 701, Yivo

Institute for Jewish Research, New York City.

26. Ronch, "The Story of the Family Circle Book," p. 157.

27. Ibid., p. 158.

28. Samuel Kreiter, "A Study of Jewish Families," *New York Times Book Review,* 3 December 1939, p. 39.

29. Henry Alsberg to Joseph Gaer, 21 July 1939, Ronch Near Print File, American Jewish Archives, Cincinnati.

30. Brehon Somervell to Isaac Rontch, Ronch Near Print File, American Jewish Archives, Cincinnati.

31. Penkower, *The Federal Writer's Project,* pp. 49–50.

32. Kreiter, "A Study of Jewish Families," p. 39.

33. Isaac Rontch to Jacob Marcus, 10 December 1979, Ronch Miscellaneous File, American Jewish Archives, Cincinnati.

34. Morris Schappes to Abe Boxerman, 29 August 1979, Ronch Miscellaneous File, American Jewish Archives, Cincinnati.

35. This claim is made by Mangione, *The Dream and the Deal,* p. 277. See also the review in Yiddish by Y. Rivkind, *Di Tsukunft* 44, no. 4 (April 1939): 239–42.

36. Henry Alsberg to Joseph Gaer, 21 July 1939, Ronch Near Print File, American Jewish Archives, Cincinnati. See also review of *These Are Our Lives* by Mary Phlegar Smith, *Social Forces* 18, no. 3 (1939): 451–52.

37. Rontch, "The Present State of the Landsmanschaften," pp. 360–78.

38. Samuel Koenig, "The Social Aspects of the Jewish Mutual Benefit Societies," *Social Forces* 18, no. 2 (1939): 274.

39. A copy of the questionnaire prepared in Yiddish for distribution to the family circles, as well as the English-language interview schedule for the Pam-Flicker Family Circle Youth Survey can be found in the Ronch Near Print File, American Jewish Archives, Cincinnati. Although the interview data for the landsmanshaftn study are not obtainable, an auxiliary source is the Works Progress Administration survey of state and local historical records. Detailed information collected by fieldworkers on the synagogues (including many landsmanshaft synagogues) in New York City is found in the WPA Historical Records Survey, Box 3751 and 3752, Municipal Archives, New York City.

40. Isaac Rontch [to meeting hall proprietors], 4 April 1940, WPA Historical Records Survey, Box 3629, Municipal Archives, New York City.

41. See memo by S.G.B., Memo evaluating chapters translated for *Jewish Landsmanschaften and Family Circles,* Federal Writers' Project Records, File A752, Manuscript Division, Library of Congress, Washington, D.C.

42. Joseph Katz, "Plan for Revision of Anglo-Jewish Book," 27, 29 November 1940, WPA Historical Records Survey, Box 3626, Municipal Archives, New York City.

43. W.K.V., "Editorial report on Landsmanshaft Societies and Family Circles (new translation)," 19 December 1940, WPA Historical Records Survey, Box 3626, Municipal Archives, New York City, p. 1.

44. Mangione, *The Dream and the Deal,* p. 334.

45. W.K.V. "Editorial report," p. 2.

46. S. H. Steinhardt to Frederick Clayton, "Jews of N.Y.," 4 September 1940, WPA Historical Records Survey, Box 3626, Municipal Archives, New York City.

47. See Charles C. Baldwin to the staff of the Jewish book, [copy of] memorandum written by H. Schneiderman of the Committee after reading a Preliminary Draft of Chapters on "Jews of New York" submitted by Kohanski, 21 August 1941; and Harry Schneiderman to Frederick Clayton, memo on Jews of New York project, 8 September 1941, WPA Historical Records Survey, Box 3633, Municipal Archives, New York City.

48. Frederick Clayton to Harry Schneiderman, memo on Jews of New York proj-

ect, 11 September 1941, WPA Historical Records Survey, Box 3633, Municipal Archives, New York City.

49. Charles Baldwin to staff of Jews of New York project, "The New York of the Jews," 24 December 1941, WPA Historical Records Survey, Box 3633, Municipal Archives, New York City, p. 1.

50. Charles Baldwin to staff on the status of the book, 6 January 1942, WPA Historical Records Survey, Box 3633, Municipal Archives, New York City.

51. Baldwin insisted that "such a study must be written objectively—without argument or special pleading . . . eliminate all superlatives." He also hastened to inform his assistants, "You may not know it, but until we took over *The Jews of New York* was largely a rewrite of other books, a rehash . . ." See Charles Baldwin, "The New York of the Jews," p. 1. Baldwin based his recommendations in part on the comments of Nathaniel Shapiro, who summarized reviews of the Federal Writers' Project book, *Italians of New York*. See Nathaniel Shapiro, "Suggestions for 'Jews of New York' based on Reviews of "Italians of New York," 3 December 1941, WPA Historical Records Survey, Box 3633, Municipal Archives, New York City, pp. 1–6.

52. See B. Z. Goldberg's review of the volume on Jewish family circles, *"Nokh a verk fun shrayber proyekt* [Another publication of the Writers' Project]," *The Day*, 11 September 1939, in Ronch Near Print File, American Jewish Archives, Cincinnati.

Part Two

Introductory Note

1. See Hannah Kliger, "That Will Make You a Good Member: The Rewards of Reading the Constitutions of Jewish Immigrant Associations," in D. Elazar, J. Sarna, and R. Monson, eds., *A Double Bond: The Constitutional Documents of American Jewry* (Lanham, Md.: University Press of America, forthcoming).

2. One set of editorial remarks about the translation claimed, "it is difficult to determine whether this is an essay on the present state of the landsmanshaft societies or a report on our project activities in gathering the data. Both techniques are mixed throughout. Writers should be less subjective . . ." See W.K.V., "Editorial report on Landsmanshaft Societies and Family Circles (new translation)," 19 December 1940, WPA Historical Records Survey, Box 3626, Municipal Archives, New York City, p. 1.

3. In one prospectus, addenda on landsmanshaft poetry and on the women's societies were proposed. See Isaac Rontch to Donald Thompson, 12 April 1938, File A752, Federal Writers' Project Records, Manuscript Division, Library of Congress.

1. The Present State of the Landsmanshaftn

1. The Yiddish phrase *"fun vanen iz a yid a landsman,"* which opens the first essay of *Di yidishe landsmanshaftn fun nyu york,* was reformulated into a literal word by word English transposition, "from whence is a Jew a *landsman*?" by Joseph Katz. His translation of this summary chapter appears as I. E. Rontch, "The Present State of the Landsmanschaften," *The Jewish Social Service Quarterly* 15, no. 4 (June 1939): 360–78, and should be consulted for a fuller representation of the Yiddish text.

2. In his introduction to the Yiddish volume, Rontch explicates the problematic development of landsmanshaft organizations, while also pointing to their as yet unfulfilled potential in contributing to Jewish life. The second subsection of the Yiddish chapter, titled "Why a book about the landsmanshaftn of New York," argues that the landsmanshaftn can be studied as "barometers of the Jewish condition in Europe and America." Federal Writers' Project, *Di yidishe landsmanshaftn fun nyu york [The Jewish Landsmanshaftn of New York].* (New York: Yiddish Writers' Union, 1938), p. 10.

3. These latter fraternal societies represent orders that were formed along political lines; they enrolled landsmanshaftn as member branches. The ideology of the Workmen's Circle stressed democratic socialism, the Jewish National Workers' Alliance combined Zionism with socialism, and the International Workers' Order, later to be renamed the Jewish People's Fraternal Order, was regulated by communist principles. Although not included in the final manuscript, a description of these and other Jewish fraternities was apparently prepared. See L. Shapiro, "Jewish Fraternal Organizations," WPA Historical Records Survey, Box 3628, Municipal Archives, New York City.

4. Here, as well as in the original Yiddish text (p. 10), the studies of Pilch and Karpf are cited. The questionnaire prepared by the Yiddish Writers' Group to remedy this situation is reproduced in the Yiddish volume (p. 12), as well as in English in I. E. Rontch, "The Present State of the Landsmanschaften," p. 363.

5. The discrepancy in the tally of family circles, which number 76 in the Yiddish publication and 112 in the English manuscript, is probably due to the discovery of additional family clubs after *Di yidishe landsmanshaftn fun nyu york* was printed in 1938, when the WPA group concentrated their efforts on the preparation of the ensuing companion volume on family circles.

6. For their survey of state and local historical records, which included synagogue records, WPA fieldworkers constructed a place name index which cross-referenced names of towns or cities in Europe with affiliated synagogues in Manhattan and other boroughs. This inventory offers important data, including date of founding, for hundreds of such landsmanshaft congregations, or ansheys, located in New York. See WPA Historical Records Survey, Box 3751 and 3752, Municipal Archives, New York City.

7. This fated meeting is detailed in a separate chapter by Berish Vaynshteyn, "*A bagegenish mitn melamed fun der alter heym* [An encounter with my teacher from the old home]," in Federal Writers' Project, *Di yidishe landsmanshaftn fun nyu york* [The Jewish landsmanshaftn of New York], 1938, pp. 123–24.

8. The Yiddish rendition that is quoted (p. 14) underscores, as well, that a specific liturgical mode and style of prayer must be followed (*"der mineg davenen darf zayn ashkenaz"*).

9. For an interesting discussion of how these practices have endured and have been adapted, see Arthur Goren, "Traditional Institutions Transplanted: The Hevra Kadisha in Europe and America," in Moses Rischin, ed., *The Jews of North America* (Detroit: Wayne State University Press, 1987), pp. 62–78.

10. Here, too, the Yiddish text (p. 14) suggests an additional explanation, namely, that in their haste to become Americanized, the younger members preferred an English designation for their society's name.

11. In the Yiddish volume (p. 14), the landsmanshaft is referred to as "a laboratory for social experimentation."

12. The Yiddish original (pp. 15–16) maintains that the rise and growth of the Jewish fraternities must undoubtedly be credited to their ability to absorb smaller societies without their autonomous landsmanshaft spirit being threatened. The 1930 annual report of the Independent Order Brith Abraham attests to the success of this strategy. Despite this, however, and despite the fact that the I.O.B.A. sprang forth from landsmanshaft societies, the leadership of the national fraternity apparently did not cooperate with the WPA in their study and, in fact, disavowed the existence of landsmanshaft-based branches within its ranks. As a result of this lack of guidance, the survey was able to identify only eighteen lodges.

13. See note 5 above regarding the total sample of family circles. In his Yiddish essay, Rontch reports that some of the family clubs were prompted to organize solely for the purpose of meeting socially on a monthly basis in order to enjoy each other's company. As the family circles are very much interested in retaining the younger

generation as active members, they have created youth leagues, cousins' clubs, and even junior leagues for children. See Federal Writers' Project, *Di yidishe landsmanshaftn fun nyu york*, 1938, p. 16.

14. In both the 1938 Yiddish version and the English translation by Joseph Katz published in the *Jewish Social Service Quarterly* in 1939 (see note 1 above), this discussion is subsumed under the separate treatment of "Language and Cultural Activities." These questions are raised again in the exchange on landsmanshaft constitutions.

15. The WPA writers also noted that the Yiddish of these handbooks shifts from an outmoded Yiddish replete with German borrowings to a more "modern Yiddish," which at the time met with disfavor on the part of landsmanshaft officers who implored: "What kind of writers are you, that we need to break our teeth on your brand of Yiddish?" See Federal Writers' Project, *Di yidishe landsmanshaftn fun nyu york*, 1938, p. 19.

16. Separate chapters are devoted to these institutions in *Di yidishe landsmanshaftn fun nyu york*, for example, David Kasher on the Moliver Home and David Sohn on the Bialystoker Center.

17. This practice of distributing charity to a variety of causes and organizations, the Yiddish writers claim, brings in mendicants of all sorts. As a result, the societies are stricter about letting outsiders into their gatherings, or they move their meetings to hotels, thus protecting themselves somewhat from "professional *pushke*-collectors." See Federal Writers' Project, *Di yidishe landsmanshaftn fun nyu york*, 1938, p. 21.

18. J. Katz renders the Yiddish text, *"nor der inhalt blaybt der zelber,"* (p. 23) as "their context remains the same," in Rontch, "The Present State of the Landsmanschaften," 1939, p. 378. In fact, the more accurate translation is not *context,* but *content.* Be that as it may, the point is that Rontch and his coworkers posited the landsmanshaft as an ever-changing structure that would transcend particular contexts or contents.

2. The Social Role of the Landsmanshaftn

1. In *Di yidishe landsmanshaftn fun nyu york,* the contribution by B. Rivkin (Weinreb) on "The Social Role of the Landsmanshaftn" is one of the longest essays (pp. 68–108), and is featured as "chapters from a larger work." This English edition, which was prepared by the WPA authors, is an abridgement of the original Yiddish text.

2. The Yiddish Writers' Group utilized *The Jewish Communal Register for 1917–1918* (New York: New York Kehillah, 1918) and M. J. Karpf, *Jewish Community Organization in the United States* (New York: Bloch Publishing Co., 1938), to substantiate their general discussion of the demographics of Jewish immigration to the United States in the nineteenth and early twentieth centuries and to correlate these population trends with landsmanshaft growth. Unless noted otherwise, the statistics in this subsection are taken from these studies.

3. The three divisions that are proposed were translated as the "synagogic-ceremonial" period up to 1905, the "nationalistic-radical" class from 1900 to World War I, and the "catastrophical" category beginning during the years of the war. In fact, these translations only approximate the meaning which the author tries to convey in his description of landsmanshaft formation, which he treats more as a continuum than as the emergence of distinct classes. In the original Yiddish essay, as well as in the English derivative, the greatest emphasis is placed on the development of the second genre, the ideological, politically-oriented orders.

4. The quintessential theme of this chapter is encapsulated here, namely that the principles of mutual aid which characterize the traditional synagogue community

have been readily and successfully embraced by nonorthodox, socially conscious groups, and that solidarity with less fortunate kin everywhere is a fundamental attribute of landsmanshaftn in America.

5. The author of this article, in noting that some Americanized Jews left their lodges to join the Elks, Eagles, Odd Fellows, and Masons, or else that others maintained membership in both organizations, indicates that participants who were dissatisfied with the narrow interests of their lodge would find this situation remedied once coalitions with national organizations were achieved. Representation in the American Jewish Committee and the American Jewish Congress, two more broad-based leagues serving larger constituencies whose histories are described, effected change in the objectives and operation of the lodges.

6. This particular passage is relayed with a dramatic flair that indicates the political convictions of members of the Yiddish Writers' Group and the New York Federal Writers' Project of which they were a part.

7. What follows is an impassioned, if sometimes unfocused, exchange on socialism, unionization, and the Americanization of the immigrant masses. Again, this interpretive exposition is a telling indicator of the worldview of this and other authors engaged by the WPA.

3. The Constitutions of the Landsmanshaftn

1. The Yiddish chapter cites, among others, the constitution of the Mezritsher Ladies' Society to exemplify the way in which landsmanshaftn adjusted and amended their by-laws "in the style of the Declaration of Independence." See Federal Writers' Project, *Di yidishe landsmanshaftn fun nyu york,* 1938, p. 43.

2. At the time of publication, the typical calendar included meetings on the first and third Sunday or the second and fourth Thursday, usually at either 8:00 or 8:30 P.M.

3. The Yiddish original (p. 46) adds that the tasks of the hospitaler include ascertaining whether the member is, in fact, really ill, and assuring that the doctor ministers to the patient properly.

4. A proviso which appears only in the Yiddish (p. 47) states that "the cost of the hat check [for the committee] will be covered by the society."

5. In the 1938 Yiddish volume (pp. 49–50), fines are noted as important sources of income for the landsmanshaftn.

6. The English translation of this particular statement does not capture the essence of the Yiddish original (p. 49) which hastily moves to add the customary wish, "*biz hundert un tsvontsik yor* [may you live to 120]," to the somber discussion which follows.

4. The Souvenir Journals of the New York Landsmanshaftn

1. While the English translation refers to sixty publications in this sample, the Yiddish chapter indicates that forty were surveyed. For examples brought from this cross section, see Federal Writers' Project, *Di yidishe landsmanshaftn fun nyu york,* 1938, pp. 158–200.

2. The Yiddish text compares the printed menus of two societies, the Kartuz-Berezer Benevolent Association and the Kartuz-Berezer Young Men's Benevolent Association, to show how "the same Berezer landslayt, in the *same* banquet hall, when they take the name 'Young Men's' (being perhaps a generation younger) prepared their menus in English (even though the souvenir journal is entirely in Yiddish). And, oh, how the 'Young Men's' must have broken their teeth on the *French* names of the courses of the meal" (p. 154).

3. It is worth noting that the souvenir journals may be seen as a predecessor to the

memorial books which would be predominantly published after World War II, offering a forum for the expression of feelings and longing for the hometown.

5. The East European Background of the Jewish Family

1. Two sections from *Yidishe familyes un familye krayzn fun nyu york*, on the foundation of the Jewish family and on Jewish immigration to America, were synthesized in the English manuscript. These source chapters, in part, help to explain the very general nature of this discussion, which also draws many of its illustrations from stereotyped portrayals of family life found in Yiddish literature. The paucity of scholarship about the Jewish family has only recently begun to be addressed, for example, in Steven M. Cohen and Paula E. Hyman, eds., *The Jewish Family: Myths and Reality* (New York: Holmes and Meier, 1986).

2. Again, I must alert the reader to the melodramatic presentation here, which more than anything else is likely a reflection of the writers' idealization of the common folk.

3. Here, the Yiddish text is much more explicit in highlighting objections to these practices. Yet, while the WPA authors find the patriarchal family system problematic in many regards, they nevertheless will claim that the defects (such as pre-arranged child marriages, or the mandate to support the studious son-in-law) simultaneously represent virtues that secure the future stability of Jewish life. See Federal Writers' Project, *Yidishe familyes un familye krayzn fun nyu york*, 1939, p. 16.

4. Remarking on this family circle, the writers seem not able to resist a sarcastic prod, at least in the Yiddish text, that "there seem to be more potential candidates for membership in this group, than for whom it would ever be possible to ascertain proper credentials" (p. 17).

5. In depicting the Jewish mother, the writers once again express their ambivalence about traditional family roles in Jewish life in the Yiddish text (pp. 20–21), but this attitude is not consistently evident in their English reproduction.

6. Jewish Family Circles

1. In the Yiddish chapter upon which this section is based, whose full title is "The Jewish Family Circle—Its Place in Organizational Life," we learn that an additional fifty-four clubs declined requests for information. See Federal Writers' Project, *Yidishe familyes un familye krayzn fun nyu york*, 1939, p. 42.

2. To introduce the family circle selected for this purpose, the Yiddish volume features the fieldnotes of one member of the project staff, Rashel Hirshkan, who observed and recorded the agenda of a meeting of the group (pp. 52–56).

3. The older members of the circle seem cognizant of the fact that to induce the active commitment of the younger generation, the group would be compelled to organize parties and dances. Yet, they concede that "these amusements are offered on a much larger and preferable scale in other organizations, where the watchful eyes of parents . . . need not be of concern." See Federal Writers' Project, *Yidishe familyes un familye krayzn fun nyu york*, 1939, p. 58. A special questionnaire was prepared and distributed to the younger contingent of the club, those between the age of twenty and twenty-six, which elicited replies from over twenty respondents regarding a variety of issues (pp. 59–60). A sample of the youth survey can be found in the Ronch Near Print File, American Jewish Archives, Cincinnati.

7. Jewish Family Life in New York City

1. In this edition, I have joined together two interconnected subheadings that appeared as divisions of Chapter III in the English typescript, and which originated from distinct chapters in the 1939 Yiddish publication.

2. This material appears as a comparative study of the older and younger generation in "Education and Culture in the Family Circle," Chapter V of Federal Writers' Project, *Yidishe familyes un familye krayzn fun nyu york*, 1939, pp. 77–92.

8. Three Generations

1. This social commentary, as it were, on the conseqences of indigence is found only in the English translation. The original Yiddish essay proceeds directly and in a more matter-of-fact manner to Neshke's biography.

2. The English manuscript makes little mention of Neshke's husband or of the couple's years together. The original text, on the other hand, dwells on her sadness in the loss of her life's companion four years prior to the writing of the book. See Federal Writers' Project, *Yidishe familyes un familye krayzn fun nyu york*, 1939, p. 103.

3. Again, we find discrepancies between the English and Yiddish versions, mainly in the longwinded description in the English chapter of Neshke's after-work involvement in her cooking preparations and her decorating hobby.

4. In the Yiddish (p. 105), far fewer details of the pogrom are reported than in the English translation. According to this Yiddish version of the drama, the children were rescued by a neighbor and were united with their father and mother only after the violence subsided.

5. The English adaptation magnifies the mother's disquietude about her son's fate rather disproportionately in comparison to the actual story line which the Yiddish writers present. In this regard, the plot that develops after Velvl's return (but only in the English draft) heightens our awareness of family relationships and the realities of Jewish domestic life.

6. The challenge here lies in transmitting the cadence of the Yiddish original while presenting passages of the English text that appear only in translation. Around this portion of the family's tale, for example, the Yiddish (p. 107) only highlights the excitement with which the clan's reunion in America was anticipated.

7. Bessie, also known as Bashe, is the subject of the entire opening presentation in the Yiddish chapter (pp. 93–102). Why this section on Neshke's sister was omitted from the English draft is unclear.

8. It is not obvious whether this sequence is a continuation of the same family saga. The names of the main characters and the general thrust of the narrative would indicate that we are dealing with component parts of the same chronicle, but some of the details do not match, as in the lines that follow: "[Isidor's] father was ailing. The mother trudged from village to town, bent under the weight of her burdensome sack, and would often be gone for days." Is this the same Neshke who worked in the cotton factory? Rontch's introductory note in the 1939 volume does not clarify this issue; it leaves open both possibilities, that each of the generational representatives derive from the same nuclear family unit, and that the individuals were chosen to be interviewed as symbols of the experiences of their contemporaries.

9. The quote, "Right here, at this kitchen table, the circle was founded in 1928," and additional particulars about Isidor's organizational commitments are in the Yiddish essay (p. 117), whereas the English text confounds the society and the family circle in which he participates, focusing only on the latter. The former, the New York Bialystoker Bikur Cholim landsmanshaft, was founded in 1897, according to I. Shmulewitz, ed., *The Bialystoker Memorial Book* (New York: The Bialystoker Center, 1982), p. 166.

10. Only the Yiddish text (p. 117) puts it this way: "She did not go to work in a shop because the number of children multiplied steadily and for many years, one might say, she was busy with her own shop."

11. In Yiddish, the text states that "Anna's job demands that she be in correspondence with hundreds of firms across America, and still she remains unpretentious,

familiar, and makes you feel as if she could be just like any young girl born in Bialystok." This last phrase appears as *"heymish, kimat a Byalistoker meydl"* (p. 122), and is certainly conveyed as a compliment to the young woman.

12. Poetic license having been employed here, the English summary introduces a different perspective on Nathan's career choice. In the Yiddish (see pp. 125–27), it is the narrator's (i.e., the project worker from the Yiddish Writers' Group) incredulity about the existence of Jewish policemen that is the major focus. The English prologue removes the disbelief from that arena and places it squarely on the subject himself, Nathan.

13. Here, too, the lack of correspondence between English and Yiddish paragraphs is telling. The Yiddish dialogue takes place in Nathan's home, in a relaxed setting at the kitchen table, with a bathrobed Nathan relating his experiences over a cup of coffee, some bread and herring. The tone of the English adaptation, I feel, assumes a greater degree of resentment, almost indignation, on his part about the course of Nathan's work life than is warranted by his own words in the Yiddish. Again, these divergences are interesting in what they may reveal about the project writers and translators.

14. Morris Rosenfeld (1862–1923) was a poet who decried the miserable conditions of workers. Sholem Aleichem (1859–1916) was the pen name of prose writer Sholem Rabinovitsh, one of the three classic writers of Yiddish literature. Moishe Nadir (1885–1943) was the pen name of Yitskhok Rayz, a popular humorist and satirist. Sholem Asch (1880–1957) was well known as a prose writer in Yiddish and in English translation. Yossel Kotler (1896–1935) was known as a humorist and cartoonist in the Communist press.

Part Three

1. Arthur Goren, *New York Jews and the Quest for Community: The Kehillah Experiment 1908–1922* (New York: Columbia University Press, 1970), p. 3.

2. Ibid., p. 2.

3. For a listing of published yisker books and excerpts from selected volumes, see Jack Kugelmass and Jonathan Boyarin, *From a Ruined Garden: The Memorial Books of Polish Jewry* (New York: Schocken Books, 1983). Additional sources on these memorial books include Philip Friedman, "Di landsmanshaftn-literatur in di fareynikte shtatn far di letste tsen yor [The past ten years of landsmanshaft literature in the United States]," *Jewish Book Annual* 10 (1951–52): 81–96; Friedman, "Monografyes fun yidishe kehiles un shtet in der yidisher geshikhte [Monographs about Jewish communities and cities in Jewish history]," in M. Bakalczuk-Felin, ed., *Yisker-bukh fun Rakishok un umgegnt (Memorial book of Rakishok and environs)* (Johannesburg: The Rakishker Landsmanshaft of Johannesburg, 1952), pp. 438–51; Elias Schulman, "A Survey and Evaluation of Yizkor Books," *Jewish Book Annual* 25 (1967–68): 184–91; Yankev Shatsky, "Yisker-bikher [Memorial books]," *Yivo Bleter* 39 (1955): 339–54; Avraham Wein, "Memorial Books as a Source for Research into the History of Jewish Communities," *Yad Vashem Studies* 9 (1973): 255–72; Annette Wieviorka and Itzhok Niborski, *Les Livres du Souvenir: Memoriaux juifs de Pologne* [The memorial books of Polish Jews] (Paris: Editions Gallimard/Julliard, 1983).

4. The selection of my sample of contemporary immigrant associations was not intended to produce a survey or even a cross section of landsmanshaftn. The absence of any one central coordinating office for these groups, as well as limitations on my access to certain societies and their officers, made it unlikely that a completely representative sample could be attained.

5. As a result of contacting various Jewish organizations and community leaders

in the New York area, a selected list of landsmanshaft leaders was assembled. The two major national Jewish philanthropic and fundraising agencies, the United Jewish Appeal and the State of Israel Bonds, have divisions that solicit funds from a variety of Jewish lodges, and they maintain the largest rosters of landsmanshaftn. I also turned to Jewish fraternal orders with branches based on locality, including the Workmen's Circle, Farband Labor Zionist Alliance, Jewish Cultural Clubs and Societies, the Independent Order Brith Abraham and Bnai Zion, and located unallied societies whose work proceeds independently and without any affiliation with other fraternities.

6. This was the case at a meeting I attended of the Workmen's Circle Warsaw-Mlaver-Tlumatcher-Rakover-Opatoshu Branch 386–639, New York, New York, 13 May 1984.

7. Czenstochauer Young Men, interview by author, tape recording, New York, New York, 25 March 1984.

8. For example, the Associated Lodzer Ladies Aid Society allocated funds in 1969 to Magen David Adom (Israel's ambulance squad), the March of Dimes, research in cancer and muscular dystrophy, and the United Jewish Appeal. See Yivo Landsmanshaftn Archive, Record Group 966, Box 1, Folder 1, Yivo Institute for Jewish Research, New York City.

9. Recent issues of *Bialystoker Shtimme* [*Voice of Bialystok*], published by the Bialystoker Center, and the Piotrkov Trybunalski Relief Association's *New Bulletin* attest to these endeavors.

10. The Council of Organizations office of the United Jewish Appeal was instrumental in bringing the masses of the American Jewish public into the Jewish fundraising arena by canvassing landsmanshaftn and other fraternal lodges. However, little information on this department is available in general histories, such as Abraham J. Karp, *To Give Life: The UJA in the Shaping of the American Jewish Community* (New York: Schocken Books, 1981), or Marc Lee Raphael, *A History of the United Jewish Appeal, 1939–82* (Chico: Scholars Press, 1982).

11. United Brahiner and Vicinity Relief Committee of Philadelphia, Box 1811, American Jewish Archives, Cincinnati.

12. Workmen's Circle Bialystoker Branch 88, interview by author, tape recording, Bronx, New York, 3 April 1984.

13. Antopoler Young Men's Benevolent Association, interview by author, tape recording, New York, New York, 10 November 1983.

14. Bialystoker Ladies Auxiliary, interview by author, tape recording, New York, New York, 14 May 1984.

15. Workmen's Circle Lodzer Women's Branch 324B, interview by author, tape recording, Bronx, New York, 7 May 1984.

16. Ochoter Warshauer Young Men's Progressive Society, interview by author, tape recording, Tarrytown, New York, 30 October 1983.

17. First Warshauer Congregation, interview by author, tape recording, New York, New York, 1 December 1983.

18. William E. Mitchell, *Mishpokhe: A Study of New York City Jewish Family Clubs* (The Hague: Mouton Publishers, 1979), pp. 84–89.

19. Marshall Sklare, foreword to William E. Mitchell, ibid., p. 9.

20. Haskell Lookstein, *Were We Our Brothers' Keepers?: The Public Response of American Jews to the Holocaust 1938–1944* (New York: Random House, 1985), p. 25.

21. For a fuller discussion, see Hannah Kliger, "In Support of Their Society: The Organizational Dynamics of Immigrant Life in the United States and Israel," in K. Olitzky, ed., *We Are Leaving Mother Russia: Chapters in the Russian-Jewish Experience in America* (Cincinnati: American Jewish Archives Press, 1990), pp. 33–53.

22. Warshauer Benevolent Society, interview by author, tape recording, Woodbridge, New Jersey, 11 October 1983.

23. Lodzer Young Men's Benevolent Society, 45th Anniversary Souvenir Journal, 1947, Yivo Landsmanshaftn Archive. Record Group 1045, Box 2, Yivo Institute for Jewish Research, New York City.

24. Bialystoker Center, interview by author, tape recording, New York, New York, 3 November 1983, 11 May 1984. In addition, I also attended the Center's Purim holiday celebration on 18 March 1984.

25. Bialystoker Bricklayers Benevolent Association, telephone interview by author, New York, New York, 11 October 1983.

26. Bialystoker Social Cutters Club, telephone interview by author, New York, New York, 11 October 1983.

27. Bialystoker Synagogue, interview by author, tape recording, New York, New York, 10 April 1984.

28. Bialystoker U. V. Somach Noflim, interview by author, tape recording, New York, New York, 15 February 1984.

29. Bialystoker Young Men's Association, interview by author, tape recording, Brooklyn, New York, 30 May 1984.

30. It proved very difficult to locate former members or to corroborate the existence of this Bialystok branch which was, however, alluded to in publications of the Bialystoker Center and of the Farband.

Bibliographic Guide

1. Milton M. Gordon, "Introduction," *Annals of the American Academy of Political and Social Science* 454 (March 1981): viii.

2. Peggy Reeves Sanday, "Cultural and Structural Pluralism in the United States," in P. Sanday, ed., *Anthropology and the Public Interest* (New York: Academic Press, 1976), p. 63.

3. William I. Thomas, *On Social Organization and Social Personality* (Chicago: University of Chicago Press, 1966), p. 210.

4. See Yaroslav J. Chyz and Read Lewis, "Agencies Organized by Nationality Groups in the United States," *Annals of the American Academy of Political and Social Science* 262 (March 1949): 148–58; S. N. Eisenstadt, *The Absorption of Immigrants* (London: Routledge and Kegan Paul, 1954); Caroline Ware, "Ethnic Communities," in *Encyclopedia of the Social Sciences* (New York: Macmillan Co., 1931), vol. 5, pp. 607–13.

5. Constance Smith and Anne Freedman, *Voluntary Associations: Perspectives on the Literature* (Cambridge: Harvard University Press, 1972).

6. Robert T. Anderson, "Voluntary Associations in History," *American Anthropologist* 73, no. 1 (February 1971): 209–22.

7. Ibid., p. 117.

8. See E. J. Dunn, *Builders of Fraternalism in America* (Chicago: The Fraternal Book Concern, 1924); B. H. Meyer, "Fraternal Beneficiary Societies in the United States," *American Journal of Sociology* 6, no. 5, (March 1901): 646–61.

9. William Kornhauser, *The Politics of Mass Society* (Glencoe: The Free Press, 1959).

10. See, for example, Floyd Dotson, "Patterns of Voluntary Association Among Urban Working Class Families," *American Sociological Review* 16, no. 5 (October 1951): 687–93; William A. Glasser and David L. Sills, *The Government of Associations* (Totowa, New Jersey: The Bedminster Press, 1966); Herbert H. Hyman and Charles R. Wright, "Trends in Voluntary Association Membership of American Adults: Replication Based on Secondary Analysis of National Sample Surveys," *American Sociological Review* 36, no. 2, (April 1971): 191–206.

11. David Knoke, "Commitment and Detachment in Voluntary Associations,"

American Sociological Review 46, no. 2, (April 1981): 141.

12. See Ferdinand Tonnies, *Community and Society* (New York: Harper and Row, 1957 edition); W. Lloyd Warner. *The Living and the Dead* (New Haven: Yale University Press, 1959).

13. Edward O. Laumann, *Bonds of Pluralism: The Form and Substance of Urban Social Networks* (New York: John Wiley and Sons, 1973).

14. Nancy Foner, ed., *New Immigrants in New York* (New York: Columbia University Press, 1987); Shirley Jenkins, ed., *Ethnic Associations and the Welfare State: Services to Immigrants in Five Countries* (New York: Columbia University Press, 1988).

15. Djuro J. Vrga, "Adjustment vs. Assimilation: Immigrant Minority Groups and Intra-Ethnic Conflict," in O. Feinstein, ed., *Ethnic Groups in the City: Culture, Institutions and Power* (Lexington: D.C. Heath, 1971), p. 40.

16. Stanford M. Lyman, "Conflict and the Web of Group Affiliation in San Francisco's Chinatown 1850–1910," in Paul Meadows and Ephraim Mizruchi, eds., *Urbanism, Urbanization and Change: Comparative Perspectives* (Reading: Addison-Wesley Publishing Co., 1976), p. 340.

17. See Djuro J. Vrga, "Adjustment vs. Assimilation," p. 45.

18. See Edward M. Bruner, "Medan: The Role of Kinship in an Indonesian City," in Bernard Farber, ed., *Kinship and Family Organization* (New York: John Wiley and Sons, 1966), pp. 88–107; Lloyd A. Fallers, ed., *Immigrants and Associations* (The Hague: Mouton and Co., 1967); P. D. Wheeldon, "The Operation of Voluntary Associations and Personal Networks in the Political Processes of an Inter-Ethnic Community," in J. Clyde Mitchell, ed., *Social Networks in Urban Situations* (Manchester: Manchester University Press, 1969), pp. 128–80. Wheeldon, for example, analyzes personal relations in a South African town, and finds that voluntary associations serve not only as focal points for the organization of specific interests or as platforms for the public expression of community needs; they are also institutions that allow those who are politically ambitious to acquire status and power.

19. John E. Bodnar, "The Formation of Ethnic Consciousness: Slavic Immigrants in Stillton," in John E. Bodnar, ed., *The Ethnic Experience in Pennsylvania* (Lewisburg: Bucknell University Press, 1973), p. 327.

20. See John E. Bodnar; Mary Bodsworth Treudley, "Formal Organization and the Americanization Process with Special Reference to the Greeks of Boston," *American Sociological Review* 14, no. 1 (February 1949): 44–53; Elena S. H. Yu, "Filipino Migration and Community Organizations in the United States," *California Sociologist* 3, no. 2 (Summer 1980): 76–102; Ivan Light, *Ethnic Enterprise in America: Business and Welfare among Chinese, Japanese and Blacks* (Berkeley: University of California Press, 1972); Richard N. Juliani, "The Origin and Development of the Italian Community in Philadelphia," in John E. Bodnar, ed., *The Ethnic Experience in Pennsylvania* (Lewisburg: Bucknell University Press, 1973), pp. 233–62.

21. Richard N. Juliani, "The Social Organization of Immigration: The Italians in Philadelphia" (Ph.D. diss., University of Pennsylvania, 1971), pp. 172–73.

22. Ibid., p. 228.

23. Jonathan Sarna, "From Immigrants to Ethnics: Toward a New Theory of Ethnicization," *Ethnicity* 5, no. 4 (December 1978): 370–78.

24. Won Moo Hurh, "Towards a Korean-American Ethnicity: Some Theoretical Models," *Ethnic and Racial Studies* 3, no. 4 (October 1980): 450–52.

25. Helena Lopata Znaniecki, "The Function of Voluntary Associations in an Ethnic Community, Polonia," (Ph.D. diss., University of Chicago, 1954); William I. Thomas and Florian Znaniecki, *The Polish Peasant in Europe and America* (New York: Dover Publications, 1938 edition).

26. Helena Lopata Znaniecki, "The Function of Voluntary Associations in an Ethnic Community," in E. Burgess and D. Bogue, eds., *Contributions to Urban Sociology* (Chicago: University of Chicago Press, 1964), p. 117.

27. Helena Lopata Znaniecki, *Polish Americans: Status Competition in an Ethnic Community* (New Jersey: Prentice Hall, 1976), p. 27.

28. Ibid., p. 25.

29. See Zachary M. Baker, "Landsmanshaftn and the Jewish Genealogist," *Toledot* 2, no. 1 (Summer 1978): 10–12; Richard L. Benkin, "Ethnicity and Organization: Jewish Communities in Eastern Europe and the United States," *Sociological Quarterly* 19, no. 4 (Autumn 1978): 614–25; Mark P. Curchak, "The Adaptability of Traditional Institutions as a Factor in the Formation of Immigrant Voluntary Associations: The Example of the Landsmanshaftn," *The Kroeber Anthropological Society Papers*, no. 42 (April 1970): 88–98; Milton Doroshkin, *Yiddish in America: Social and Cultural Foundations* (Cranbury: Associated University Presses, 1969), pp. 136–69. In addition, see the special issue devoted to landsmanshaftn in *American Jewish History* 76, no. 1 (September 1986).

30. Isaac Levitats, "The Jewish Association in America," in Joseph Blau et al., eds., *Essays in Jewish Life and Thought Presented in Honor of Salo Wittmayer Baron* (New York: Columbia University Press, 1959), pp. 348–49.

31. See Karl Applebaum, "A History of the Jewish 'Landsmanshaftn' Organizations in New York City," (M.A. thesis, New York University, 1952); Myra Giberovitsh, "The Contributions of Montreal Holocaust Survivor Organizations to Jewish Communal Life," (M.A. thesis, McGill University School of Social Work, 1988); Miriam Hoffman, "Memory and Memorial: A Survey into the Making of a *Yizker-bukh*," (M.A. thesis, Columbia University, 1983); Susan Milamed, "Proskurover Landsmanshaftn: A Case Study in Jewish Communal Development," (M.A. thesis, Columbia University, 1980); Daniel Soyer, "Between Two Worlds: The Landsmanshaftn and Questions of Immigrant Identity," (M.A. Thesis, New York University, 1985); William E. Mitchell, *Mishpokhe: A Study of New York City Jewish Family Clubs* (The Hague: Mouton Publishers, 1978); Michael R. Weisser, *A Brotherhood of Memory: Jewish Landsmanshaftn in the New World* (New York: Basic Books, 1985).

32. Maxwell Whiteman, "Western Impact on East European Jews: A Philadelphia Fragment," in Randall Miller and Thomas D. Marzek, eds., *Immigrants and Religion in Urban America* (Philadelphia: Temple University Press, 1977), p. 121.

33. Irving Howe, "Pluralism in the Immigrant World," in David Berger, ed., *The Legacy of Jewish Migration: 1881 and its Impact* (New York: Columbia University Press, 1983), p. 152.

34. See, for example, Jeffrey Gurock, *When Harlem Was Jewish 1870–1930* (New York: Columbia University Press, 1979); Irving Howe, *World of Our Fathers* (New York: Harcourt Brace Jovanovich, 1976); Paula Hyman, "Immigrant Women and Consumer Protest: The New York City Kosher Meat Boycott of 1902," *American Jewish History* 70, no. 1 (September 1980): 91–105; Deborah Dash Moore, *At Home in America: Second Generation New York Jews* (New York: Columbia University Press, 1981); William Toll, "'The New Social History' and Recent Jewish Historical Writing," *American Jewish History* 69, no. 3 (March 1980): 315–41.

35. See Josef Korazim, "Immigrant Associations in Israel," in Shirley Jenkins, ed., *Ethnic Associations and the Welfare State*, 1988, pp. 155–202; L. Losh, ed., *Landsmanshaftn in yisroel* [Landsmanshaftn in Israel] (Tel Aviv: Association of Jews from Poland, 1961); Zvi Porat-Noy, ed., *Sefer hashana lekehilot ve'irgunim yehudi'im 1983* [Yearbook of Jewish communities and organizations 1983] (Ramat Gan, 1983); M. Tsanin, *Tsen yor medines yisroel* [Ten years of the State of Israel] (Tel Aviv: Letste Nayes, 1958).

36. See Hannah Kliger, "Ethnic Voluntary Associations in Israel," *Jewish Journal of Sociology* 31, no. 2 (December 1989): 109–19; Jonathan Boyarin, "Landslayt: Polish Jews in Paris," (Ph.D. diss., New School for Social Research, 1985). The over 400 published memorial books contain information about landsmanshaft activities in communities throughout the world, including Israel, Canada, Mexico, South America, Australia, South Africa, and Europe.

INDEX

Affiliation: family circles as outgrowth of landsmanshaft model, 120; modifications of landsmanshaft model, 126–28

Age: members of benefit organizations, 36; Americanization, 36–37; dues of new members, 62. *See also* Children; Elderly

Aid: role of landsmanshaftn, 40–41. *See also* Mutual aid; Sick-benefit societies

American Gathering of Jewish Holocaust Survivors: partnership with Bialystoker Center, 130

Americanization: age and members, 36–37; theater benefits, 39; social role of landsmanshaftn, 52, 53; Jewish socialism, 56; portrayal of second-generation immigrant, 109–10, 112; English society names, 149; participation in landsmanshaftn and other organizations, 151; worldview of WPA authors, 151

American Jewish Committee: objectives, 53

American Jewish Congress: compared to American Jewish Committee, 53; social power of landsmanshaftn, 57

Ansheys: types of landsmanshaftn, 31–32; religion and social role of landsmanshaftn, 49

Anti-Semitism: B'nai B'rith, 45; economic status of youth, 91; portrayal of second-generation immigrant, 110, 111

Arts: cultural status of native-born Jewish youth, 98–99

Asch, Sholem: class struggle, 55

Authorship: publications of Yiddish Writers' Group, 5–6, 146

Baldwin, Charles: plans for English volume, 15; criticism of *The Jews of New York,* 148

Banks, Ann: on Federal Writers' Project, viii

Bar mitzvah: constitutions of congregational societies, 66

Benevolent societies: function of landsmanshaftn, 11; differentiated from landsmanshaftn, 27; death compensation, 49

Bialystoker Center: information on contemporary landsmanshaftn, 128–30

Bialystoker Unterstitzungs Verein Somach Noflim: older traditions of landsmanshaft life, 129

Bialystoker Young Men's Association: continuities of landsmanschaftn, 129

B'nai B'rith: social role of landsmanshaftn, 44–45

B'rith Abraham: landsmanschaft branches of fraternal orders, 34; social role of landsmanshaftn, 45, 53; death compensation, 49; development of orders, 50; establishment of HIAS, 54

Broder Young Men's Benevolent and Educational Alliance: data on members, 35

Brotherhood: attempts to unite landsmanshaftn, 42

Charities: role of landsmanshaftn, 40–41; religious nature of landsmanshaftn, 49; social power of landsmanshaftn, 57; postwar landsmanshaftn, 122; outsiders and limitations on, 150. *See also* Aid; Mutual aid; Sick-benefit societies

Children: age at first employment, 88; Eastern European Jewish family life, 73; Jewish family life in New York City, 89. *See also* Age

Class: social role of landsmanshaftn, 51–53, 55; family circles, 77–78, 81. *See also* Middle class; Working class

Clayton, Frederick: plans for English volume, 15

College: educational status of native-born Jewish youth, 98; portrayal of third-generation immigrant, 113–14

Communism: accusations against Yiddish Writers' Group, 7–8

Community: role of landsmanshaftn, 27–28; role of sick-benefit societies, 33; Jewish family life, 71

Congregational societies: constitutions compared to landsmanshaft, 58, 65–66

Constitutions: landsmanshaftn, 58–66; family circles, 78–79

Culture: landsmanshaft activities, 38–40; landsmanshaftn and transmission of, 119

The Day (Der tog): survey on importance of immigrant associations, 3; articles on landsmanshaft activities, 127

Death: compensation and social role of landsmanshaftn, 49; mourning and sick benefits, 64; constitutions, 64–65; cemeteries and Jewish family circles, 77, 79–80; continuities in landsmanshaftn, 121

Depression, Great: economic status of youth, 90–91; educational status and occupation of native-born Jewish youth, 98, 114

Dies, Martin: criticism of Yiddish Writers' Group, 8

Dues: age of new members, 62

Dutch landsmanshaftn: dates of founding, 35